Otto, The M

CW01429825

80 Long Years to Learn 40 Short Lessons

Peter "Otto" Abeles

Tom "Hickey" Hicks

Rodney "Clyde" Pickel

Peter Otto Abeles

Otto's Lessons

For Openers

You always learn something even if you don't know it

My name is Peter "Otto" Abeles. I was born in Vienna, Austria in 1931. This past year I turned 80 years old. I have some unfinished business to complete in this book. My friend, Tom Hicks was the co-author of my first book written ten years ago entitled <u>Otto, the Boy at the Window</u>. Tom and I explored in that book the true story of how I escaped the Holocaust and started a new life in America despite a lot of obstacles. Tom is a dear friend and a long time business partner and we have had many adventures together though we come from two totally different worlds. That is the beauty of America.

We have teamed up with Rodney Pickel, another close friend whom I will often refer to affectionately as Clyde. That was his nickname as a boy and it fits him well. Clyde portrayed me beautifully in the play we produced about my story and I thought it only fitting that he work with Tom and me to finish telling it. You will find his insight special and his experiences diverse. Clyde calls Tom by his childhood nickname, Hickey. So there you have it in a nutshell, Otto, Hickey, and Clyde, three friends coming together for a special purpose.

Please join this eclectic group as we share 40 short simple lessons learned in my 80 years of living on this planet. Each lesson is condensed into a short chapter for you to ponder. Both friends have expressed their views of these lessons and their application to business and life in general and we close each chapter with a quip and an image. The illustrations are the creative work of David Prothro and Joey Pruitt who somehow figured out how to read our minds.

In my original book, the account delved into my experiences with emotional child abuse and the important message of forgiveness. Nashville playwright Bill Dorian adapted the entire story into a stage production that made its very successful debut in 2007 and was brought back in 2009. As I shared earlier, Rodney Pickel narrated the story playing me in the present day. It is amazing to see your life unfold before you on the stage and as I thought about it additional stories popped into my mind.

For some time now, I knew there was much more to tell and I have wanted to continue the narrative of my journey here in America. In conversations with Tom and Rodney, we formed a plan to add the character Otto to their project, Bungalow, the Adventures of Hickey and Clyde. They were exploring friendship and the concept of finding your way *home*. But one thing leads to another. That's how life works. For shortly into the process, a new idea was born. Why not create a whole new book based on the many lessons I have learned, particularly in business? Though we think our idea is brilliant for there isn't a shortage of ego in this group but I must confess it really came from the beautiful and talented Nashville singer and actress, Janna Landry. Her thought was, since *Hickey and Clyde* was almost completed; why not center a new story on Otto? As I considered that possibility, an image popped into my head. It was clear to me. Thus, *Otto, The Man at the Wheel*, emerged, driving a Waste Management garbage truck through a line of student protesters in the 1960's on a busy street in Madison, Wisconsin.

As I share some important education learned in the school of hard knocks and some amusing stories over these next several pages, I will often refer to the influence of my old friends or perhaps I will reference my new friends like Kinky Friedman, who I may refer to as the Kinkster, not to mention a whole host of other unique characters I've encountered over the years as I've made this incredible journey on this rock called Earth.

Although my relationship with my father was certainly far from ideal, he was the example of the kind of businessman I wanted to be. Before the Nazi's stole his livelihood, he had been chosen as Vienna's "Business Man of the Year" in 1936. He was an entrepreneur. That's what I wanted to be. You see at the age of 80, I am no longer a little boy at the window watching others control my life. I am the man at the wheel, driving the truck that carries all of my life's lessons in it. In the ensuing short chapters join me as I steer through the curves and accelerate up the hills and even brake when something gets in my way. But trust me, I do not stop for anything and as I look in my rear view mirror from time to time it is only to see where I've been. Because in this life if you don't watch where you're going you will most certainly run off the road and we all know where that ends up.

Join me on a short trip through the years of my life and the miles of my experiences and perhaps you will learn a little something that will help you on your own journey. But like me, you will find that beyond the next bend there are always a few surprises and some interesting people. As my grandmother, Pipin used to say, "What I have lived through I know. What I am going to live through only God knows." It is an old Jewish saying that "God could not be everywhere and therefore he made Grandmothers". How true that is.

3

As with any project, the first question is how would we put this thing together?

So there we each sat at our offices miles away from each other thinking about the number 40. Don't ask me how it came up? It just did. We are all big on brainstorming and coming up with fresh ideas. We are also big believers in fate. We never underestimate the value of hard work but we still think there are bigger forces at work.

So what is the meaning of the number forty or 40, if that's how you choose to write it, in our lives? Tom and Clyde and I had determined that our new book would have 40 concise chapters each with a lesson about what I had discovered in these eight decades.

A lot of what we as Jews and Christians have learned come from the Bible. So Tom did some research and when he reported back, it all made sense to me. Astonishingly a time period of 40 (days, weeks, years, people, places, events) is in fact noteworthy. From biblical perspective most if not all time periods of 40 units are related to testing, experimentation or being tried. Also and this is where the reward kicks in, each period ends with a time or item of blessing. Since I feel my life has been a blessing despite the setbacks, this seemed like a logical place for me to start.

Otto the Philosopher's #1 Workplace Commandment
"*This office is a No Whine Zone!*"

Chapter 1
There is a blessing beyond belief

As business owners and entrepreneurs, you learn to do it all. Tom and I have delivered parts and made service calls to get paid at all times of the day and night. When you are in charge of customer relations, it is important to be right but is most important to get paid. In the end, that is really what counts. But, boys will be boys and like the song "Girls Just Wanna Have Fun", so do boys. I mean, really want to have fun.

The four years I spent in the United States Air Force was an important part of my life and a great learning experience. It was a lot of hard work and during that time I had to learn that someone else was behind the wheel and I was just supposed to follow orders. That is hard to do for an independent guy like myself.

I found out that if you did the crime you had to do the time as Tony Beretta would say. It was Sunday afternoon, our only day off and as my buddies and I scanned the bulletin board, the first thing we saw was Monday's KP roster. Lo and behold my name was on top of the list, which of course made sense, since the list was in alphabetical order. Four of my buddies were also so honored, so we made big plans for our day off. Like all red-blooded American boys we decided to party that night. We splurged and went to a fine restaurant and of course, graced the premises of all our favorite hang outs. Late that night this group of worn out Air Force boys called it quits and headed back to the base. Feeling no pain, I might add. On the journey back, we spotted a drive-in, shut down for the night, with a huge sign out front declaring "Closed on Mondays". Despite my altered state, a brilliant idea popped into my head. "Stop", I yelled! "Take a look at that sign! I have an idea. Why don't we steal the sign and hang in front of the mess hall?"

Today I am reminded of something Clyde's old pal Mike Mountain used to say, "No air battle, no medal." That'll make more sense later. Trust me.

Anyway, back to my story. It's not hard to get a carload of drunken guys to agree to anything. I recommend if you have a brilliant idea and your inebriated pals agree with you, perhaps before you act, you might want to wait until you sleep on it to determine its genius. But, since it was very late and there would be no one near the mess hall, we carefully hung the sign where it was prominently displayed in clear view.... and went to bed. Early the next morning we reported for KP duty as scheduled. Every one wondered why the five of us all had stupid grins on our faces. At 6 a.m. the Mess Sergeant opened the doors for breakfast and of course nobody showed up. At 6:30 a.m., coincidentally, there was a phone call from the other mess hall and an agitated voice reported, "We are swamped. What the hell is goin' on?" Somebody went outside and spotted the sign and reported it to the Mess Sergeant whose face turned crimson red. Well the shit hit the fan and that's never a very pretty picture. He took one look at the group of us and apparently had no trouble narrowing it down to the fabulous five. After a severe tongue lashing that ranked up there with one of my mother's rages after tripping over my toy soldiers; we got a week of KP as our punishment. Though I didn't feel it at the time, I have to say, it was worth it.... in many ways. It bonded my friendship with my other buddies, and it also taught me, really taught me, there are always consequences for your actions. Beretta was right.

Later in the business world when I was first starting out, my father and I had another of our ongoing arguments. Working for family *can* be rewarding but it can also be very stressful. This particular argument was different and far more violent. In life, battles are a part of the deal. I learned that lesson as a child in Vienna when the Nazis came rolling into town. You see, I respected my father, but this was a different time and place. It was obvious I wasn't going to win this battle with him so, to make our long argument short, I quit. My father told me I couldn't quit.....then he proceeded to fire me. And, that was ok with me except for this one thing that really pissed me off... he took my company car.

As I rode home on the train, angry and scared, I formed a plan of action. I like to write down my plans and so I scribbled my thoughts to the rhythm of the rails.

I needed some wheels so *Item 1* was *Look for any kind of job as long as it provides a company car.* I was on a roll now and *Item 2* came quickly. *Use the new company car on my day off to look for a better paying and more permanent job. Item 3* was the culmination of the two, *Sky's the Limit!* I had a lot of confidence in myself and recommend that you have the same. If you are not your #1 Fan, then who is?

After scanning the "help wanted ads" for a few days, I came across something interesting. It read, *"Collector messenger wanted- company car provided- Contact Ace Scavenger Company".* I copied down the address. Ace Scavenger Company was a large trash collection company. When I applied for the job, I told them I didn't just *need* the job, I *wanted* the job. My confident, positive attitude paid off. While proudly driving home in my new company car I was reminded of *Item 1* in my plan. *Look for any kind of job as long as it provided a company car.* Step 1 complete. The soldier in me was winning. Remember, "No air battle, no medal".

The job entailed servicing what they called their cash collection routes each day. I would visit their customers in different parts of the city and collect the fees they owed for the services we provided. The job was easy, *and* kind of boring, but as I looked around on my routes I found a lot of businesses that seemed to have no collection service. And, as it just so happens, there was a lot of construction going on in those days. Don't be discouraged, my friends, because America's construction business will come back to life. It has in the past and will in the future.

That afternoon I asked my boss if he would mind if I tried soliciting new business for the company. Not only did he not mind, he was delighted! He promised the first month's charge from any new account as my commission. I was so excited I could hardly sleep that night. I tried counting sheep but all I saw was dollar signs.... $$$$. You see, and here's part of the lesson, if you visualize money first, then you already have it in a way and you can start claiming it for your own. As Napoleon Hill said, "There is one quality which one must possess to win, and that is definiteness of purpose, the knowledge of what one wants, and a burning desire to possess it." I knew what I wanted and I had a burning desire to possess it.

The next day I started looking for new accounts, first small stores, then gas stations and finally parking lots. Soon I was bringing in new customers every week. I loved the commission checks. After a few months, I asked the boss if I could get some help with the collections so I could have more time to develop new customers. He loved it! The way I see it, if you don't have new ideas popping into your head every day, then something's wrong. They should be pouring in at the same rate as the commission checks. So, formulate these ideas into plans and take action. And remember just as there are negative consequences for negative actions, there are positive consequences for positive actions. "For whatsoever a man soweth, that shall he also reap."

On a side note, I also learned a very valuable business lesson from a completely different perspective. You see my boss, Dean Buntrock, began to realize my sales efforts were paying off, both for me and the company. Consequently, he decided that weekly sales meetings were in order. As he and I became more comfortable with each other, Mr. Buntrock began to share his business problems and concerns with me. Therein lies the birthplace of my new idea and the reason for this "side note". As he listed things he either did not like to do or had no time to do, I would offer to take care of them for him. For a lazy man, this might be considered "sucking up", but for a man with high aspirations it was merely an opportunity to begin a path down the road of entrepreneurship. You see, one of the steps to succeeding within the company structure, is to find out what's on your bosses' "don't like" list, and make that your personal "to do" list. Trust me; it works. Now, where was I? Oh yeah…..

The next day I came to work wearing a white shirt and conservative tie and announced proudly, "I am going to start looking for some large customers." I hadn't forgotten all that new construction going on. You see, growth stimulates and inspires a *salesman.* The folks in the office were somewhat surprised at the sight of me in my new wardrobe. That's because they had never seen anyone dressed up in the *trash* business. I spent evenings at the library and started poring over the Dodge Report. I made a note to myself to convince the boss to let me subscribe to this useful tool. These reports listed every new building and factory under construction.

I was not afraid to ask questions. I was not afraid to make mistakes. When you are at the bottom, every fall is a short one.

Slowly at first, I started having success. And soon, my commission checks were much bigger than my salary. It wasn't long before I had a title *and* an office. My new career had started out of the ashes of my old one. The cars got nicer, the titles more prestigious and the offices bigger. Eventually I became an officer of Waste Management. I am reminded of a saying of another old friend of my pal Clyde's. His name was Bob Cahill and he lived in Northern California. He used to say, "In order to accumulate, you got to speculate." I guess you could say my speculations were starting to pay off.

As it turned out, I never really had to incorporate *Item 2.* It happened in its own time. *Item 3* is still happening. *Sky's the limit!* If I were to summarize, I would say this. Whatever you do, you should do it to the hilt whether playing a prank or starting a new career, do it with the same gusto. In other words, play hard and work hard. Certainly, winning is about the prize, but it is also about the battle, large or small, and the pleasure in knowing you gave it all you had, and being able to say "I did it; I fought the good fight, I finished the course, and I kept the faith."

And, I've got to tell you, it feels good! You should always practice the art of "feeling good". And, what adds to that feeling and makes it even better, and this is the really cool part, is taking what you have learned and being able to say, "I helped someone else do it, too!" Why the hell not? Be the patron you were destined to be.

And therein lies the wonderful law of exponents, when you hear that the person you helped do it helps someone else do it and the third party doesn't even know you were involved. That is *the blessing beyond belief,* living life on your own terms, the very best of terms, at the top of the heap where the air is fresh and clean.

"Gentlemen, Otto's terms are simple...
I accept only unconditional surrender!"

Chapter 2
Life starts with a few stutter steps

Nobody and I mean nobody has it easy. Everyone has a few curses to go with their blessings. It's called being human. You stumble around. Walking itself has been described as a controlled fall. Let me explain.

My wife Bonnie and I had the chance to see the Academy Award winning film, *The King's Speech*. The unlikely monarch, King George VI of Britain, was brilliantly portrayed by Colin Firth, who won both the Oscar and Golden Globe for Best Actor. It's also worth mentioning that Geoffrey Rush in the role of the speech therapist was also outstanding. Although nominated for Best Supporting Actor, he lost out to another amazing performance by Christian Bale in *The Fighter*. But, I digress. Back to *The King's Speech*, I have to admit that as great as the movie was, it brought back painful memories of my freshman year in High School. You see, that's when I began to stutter, and for a fourteen year old kid from Vienna, Austria living in Chicago, that can be devastating. In a nutshell, it made my life miserable.

Quite frankly, a stuttering freshman is not just subject to ridicule, but will most likely attract the attention of the school bully. In those days, bullying in school was not only tolerated, but often completely overlooked. And, that left only two options. Either suck it up.... or do something about it. I was reading just the other day that more than 68 million people worldwide stutter, which is about 1% of the population. In the

15

United States, that's over 3 million Americans who stutter. So, I wasn't alone. But of course, I didn't know that then.

Now, you would expect a young guy like me, who'd only been in America for 7 years, would get a little support from his family. But, then again, you didn't know my family. Apparently my mother thought that *stuttering* was a defect and since she couldn't trade me in for a better model, she dealt with me the only way she knew how. She would shake me, as though that would erase the pressure of stammering, and yell "Speak right, Otto!"

As you might imagine, her *help* was ineffective. In fact, research also shows that family problems, of which we had more than our share, may in fact contribute to stuttering and stammering. This shaking routine occurred whenever my actions were considered an infraction by mother's standards. Eventually, I began to fear all physical human contact. Whenever anyone would wrap their arms around me, for *whatever* reason, I expected to be shaken violently. It even terrorized me to be hugged. Can you imagine the emotional and physical problems resulting from not wanting to be hugged?

Well, since Mother's corrective method was not having the desired effect, I decided I had to solve the problem on my own. As always Heinz Robert, my older brother was there to help and together we developed a plan. Rather than just sitting and reading the paper quietly and to myself, I would stand in front of the mirror and read stories from the Chicago Tribune aloud, over and over until I was flawless. Guess what. It worked.

Eventually the stuttering stopped, and since I was no longer stuttering, so did the shaking. Slowly, I warmed up to the idea of being touched and began to see it as a positive thing. Tom and Clyde are both huggers and whenever we see each other; *just guess what we do?* You got it. We hug! It's awkward at first but you kind of get used to it and then you desire it. And the old proverb says "as you teach you learn."

You see, one thing leads to another and before long you might not even remember when or why you got off track. So what do you do? Do what I did. Take the bull by the horns and develop a strategy that gets the job done. And the unintended consequences of a *negative* circumstance can have unexpected *positive* results.

For me, I learned to overcome my speech problem, became a better reader, knew more about the news events that shaped my world, and rediscovered the beauty of a hug. And when I saw the movie about the king who had similar problems and through the help of an honest though unlikely friendship working toward a lifelong solution, I realized that everyone is in the same boat. That recognition helped make me a better marketing professional for business and that personal experiences can't be compartmentalized. Bottom line.... relating to the weaknesses of others strengthens our own efforts.

On my bulletin board at my home office, I have a valuable saying located where I can see it at all times. It reads: *If you can't eliminate stress, learn to manage it.*

I still don't like shaking as much as hugging unless it is a method used to make a perfect martini. And when there is one of those tasty treats around, Clyde and Hicks will always be around to join me. So you see, I took a negative and turned it into a toast to celebrate life. L'Chaim!

You are the one and only reflection of who you really
are and who you will one day be.

Chapter 3
Mobsters are People, Too

In the summer of 1949 I decided to apply for a job driving a Checker Cab. Little did I know that to be a "cabbie" I would have to become a member of the local trade union. This was, after all, the Chicago I had heard about as a boy in Vienna and was now a reality to me. I filled out all the necessary paperwork and was told by the clerk that the fee was sixty bucks! To me at the time, sixty dollars was a small fortune! She might as well have asked for a million.

As I stood there, tearfully explaining to the nice lady that I did not have the funds, a short dapper looking man walked by the counter. He must have overheard my sad story. He stopped and reached into his pocket. For all I knew he was about to pull out a gun. This *was* Chicago and I recalled those images of the gangster movies I loved as a young boy in Austria. Heinz Robert used to play the role of Al Capone and I was his muscle. We would ride with Adolph, our chauffeur, through the streets of Vienna pretending to be the mob. We had so much to learn.

Anyhow, the man pulled out a huge wad of cash and peeled off three crisp twenty dollar bills. He said "Here kid. Pay me back from your first pay check." Then he spun on his heels and disappeared into the office. I stood there stunned, grateful of course, but stunned nonetheless. Finally I heard the nice lady clearing her throat to get my attention. So, I handed her the money. She seemed a little surprised by the actions of the man with the wad of money. "Do you know who that was?" she asked.

I shook my head and managed to get out a muffled "no".

"That was Joey Glimco, the president of the union. If I were you, I would pay back the money as soon as possible or you will end up with some broken bones." She grimaced at me and I got the message loud and clear.

I mumbled thanks and rushed out of the office looking over my shoulder to make sure the door to the office remained closed. I walked quickly down the street hoping I wasn't being tailed.

With my first check, I immediately paid off my sixty dollar debt. I loved being a cabbie. I learned a lot about the city that I now consider my home. Joseph Paul Glimco died in 1991. That was a memorable day for me. He was an Italian American labor leader and the union did a lot for the working stiffs in The Windy City. He was also a well-known organized crime figure. He was considered "Chicago's top labor racketeer" in the 1950s. One high-ranking Chicago Teamsters leader noted in 1954, "He is the mob. When he opens his mouth, it's the syndicate talking." Glimco was active in the International Brotherhood of Teamsters (IBT) and a close associate of Teamsters president Jimmy Hoffa. I really can't speak to all of that.

All I know personally of Joey Glimco is that he helped out a kid who really needed it, a kid who was able and more than willing to repay the loan. But, he did something else. He gave me a break. He didn't have to do that. You can be as independent as you want in this world. You can say you do things on your own, but now and then, everyone needs a break, from the janitor to the CEO. And, if there is one thing we need to remember, it is to be grateful. That man changed my life.

Tom often tells me that I am his business mentor. He says we were brought together by destiny and that he is eternally thankful that we were. Out of that relationship, my first book was spawned, *Otto the Boy at the Window*. Then out of the blue, we both seemed to be inspired at the same time. That inspiration led to a stage version of my life. We contracted William Dorian, a Nashville director and brilliant playwright to develop a theatrical production for us. I remember the day Tom told me that Rodney Pickel was perfect to portray me as an adult on stage. We then brought him into the mix for his superb acting talents.

Like the dream I had the day I walked into Mr. Glimco's office, I know there is more to be done. Dreams and people are both meant to be fulfilled. It takes gratitude, but it also involves something else. And that is old fashioned hard work. I like to think when Joey Glimco saw me standing there he had a gut feeling that this kid had what it took. I like to think that I come across as someone who has been around the block, chased by Nazis and haunted by my childhood memories of a volatile home life. I like to think I'm a guy who takes advantage of every opportunity, no matter where it comes from. I guess you could say I like to think.

And thinking requires a price, your valuable time. When someone says "a penny for your thoughts", you might consider negotiating because they are worth a lot more and your actions even more for as the old sages thought, "If charity cost nothing, the world would be full of philanthropists." Be a real humanitarian. A mobster was to me.

"Just remember, kid, nobody's all bad.
Not even you or me."

Chapter 4
Do the Things you Fear
and Never Fear the Things You Do

One weekday morning, scores of years ago, I was sitting in my office in Madison, Wisconsin trying to catch up on some paper work. I liked to keep up with the news, so I typically had the radio on when I was in my office. News of the Vietnam War filled the airwaves. This conflict began in 1955 and didn't end until 1975. The U.S. government viewed its involvement as a way to prevent a communist takeover of South Vietnam.

The war escalated in the early 1960s, with U.S. troop levels tripling in 1961 and tripling again in 1962. U.S. combat units were deployed beginning in 1965, and peaked in 1968. U.S. Military involvement finally ended on August 15, 1973. The capture of Saigon by the North Vietnamese army in April 1975 marked the end of the Vietnam War. There are some estimates that over three million Vietnamese soldiers and civilians were killed and as many as 300,000 Cambodians and 200,000 Laotians. The Vietnam War cost 58,220 U.S. service members their lives. Hearing news of this war on a daily basis brought back horrible memories of my early life in Vienna, Austria. I was so grateful to be on U.S soil and living the American Dream.

Early that morning my phone rang. The panicked voice on the other end of the line said, "Hey Boss we are stuck downtown. The demonstrators have my truck surrounded." It's amazing how much this war was rattling the emotions of our citizens. The anti-war movement in the United States began with demonstrations in 1964 and grew in strength in later years. Opposition groups sprang from the Civil Rights Movement and the anti-nuclear movement, among others. These groups were comprised largely of college and graduate students; mothers, and the anti-establishment hippies. Usually their demonstrations were peaceful, but occasionally turned violent. "I will be there as soon as possible", I told my man on the other end. I grabbed my hat and coat and rushed out the door, not knowing what I was about to face.

As I was driving downtown I began to develop a plan of action. Thoughts raced through my mind, each one informing the next until one thought finally stopped the race. It was something John F. Kennedy had recently said. His most famous quote was one we all remember. "And so, my fellow Americans, ask not what your country can do for you; ask what you can do for your country." Being a veteran myself, this quote certainly held special meaning, but the one I had recently heard was most appropriate for the current circumstances. And it was, "Do not pray for easy lives. Pray to be stronger men." Since I anticipated an uneasy situation, I simply prayed for strength.

When I reached my downtown destination, I parked my car and walked over to our truck. I immediately sized up the situation. The anti war demonstration was so large the demonstrators had inadvertently surrounded the truck. I made my decision. I really didn't know what to expect. The situation was most likely *not* a dangerous one, but I really didn't know that. This was certainly no time for fear. Ralph Waldo Emerson said, "Do the thing you fear, and the death of fear is certain." I snatched the keys from the driver, got in the truck, and started the engine. I figured the demonstrators were only concerned with their cause and not with the vehicle. I inched the truck slowly forward. Nobody moved. I thought perhaps I had misjudged the situation. Then I remembered my resolve. "Stick to your plan and keep driving." Slowly the crowd began to move and finally the truck was past the demonstrators. The driver was impressed with my bravery. Had he known how scared I really was, I doubt my actions would have made the same impression. It was, I guess, a small act of "fake it 'til you make it".

Hemingway spoke of courage as "grace under pressure". A man has to suck it up sometimes and keep his game face on. Martin Luther King, a champion of human rights during that volatile time in American History kept his "eyes on the prize" and it cost him his life. But I believe that if given the choice he would do it all over again because he knew his legacy of courage would matter to millions.

Tom thinks the greatest fear in life is the trepidation concerning death. He maintains that even fear can be removed when you cease to think that building wealth is the only objective instead of a healthy reward.

He asserts that you must become a real person to your family and co-workers and even for those who don't know you, it is important that you embark on a mission to define your legacy. This begins by keeping a written or digital journal and a photo chronology of your experiences and particularly your milestones.

A compilation of what you did coupled with an explanation of why you did it gives those who come after you a guidepost as they climb their own mountains and fight their own battles.

Further, it is important to think. Most people don't like to be alone and many of those don't like to think and often are fearful of the whole process of self-evaluation. Set aside time for the experience of reflection, then define those ideas and plans and put them into action both as short term objectives and as a long term goal of building a heritage that demonstrates you as an individual but also as a part of the advancement of your family, your business and as a result all humankind.

Clyde selects his roles as an actor with great care. He wants to demonstrate his acting ability but equally important he wants to make a statement in his unique way, be it in the form of a comedy or the intensity of jurors making a life and death decision in 12 Angry Men. When Tom and I were thinking about who could effectively portray me in the stage version of our book, we selected Clyde as we said earlier because of his acting ability of course, but equally important because of his passion.

That day back in the 60's has long since passed. Many of the people in that crowd are still alive and fulfilling their version of the American Dream and some probably reflect upon that same day and what happened to them in a completely different way.

I am still here and grew immensely from that event just like they did. What we each do with our experiences is what shapes our lives. Yep, I was driving that truck and my fear was turned into an impulse to grab the keys and just drive. Just do my job. In the end, we have to listen to our gut feelings and then act on them. In the vernacular of that era, "Let it all hang out."

Looking back, I see a great lesson. The things in life we fear are like the chains that bind us. Until we unlock and remove those chains, we are destined to a life of failure. Until we face and conquer our fears, we're doomed to a life of mediocrity. Remember the words of Ralph Waldo Emerson. "Do the thing you fear, and the death of fear is certain." I certainly agree.

The key to economics, business, and life is simple. Treat everyone like your best customer. Smile and say thank you as you make a tidy little profit and they get something they want. We have one thing in common. As I tell Tom every time we are together, "Everyone likes to buy shit."

"
Peace is cool, man.
But a piece of the action isn't bad either!"

Chapter 5
Quid Pro Quo -
Home Runs On and Off the Field

After escaping Vienna, Austria on the last boat leaving, my family and I landed in Chicago in December 1939. Chicago is a great sports town and one of its most notable landmarks is Wrigley Field. Since I loved baseball from the first time I played it, *and* Wrigley Field from the first time I saw it, it was only natural that I was destined to be a Cub fan. Say what you want about the Cubs and their curse, it is a great organization and has graced its cathedral with some of the best to ever play the game. Wearing the Big C has included such hall of famers as Ernie Banks, Fergie Jenkins, Ryne Sanberg, and Billy Williams. Not to mention a few who were known primarily as Cardinals, like Lou Brock, Dizzy Dean, and Rogers Hornsby. My friend, Clyde, bleeds Cardinal Red and he and I have a healthy competitive rivalry, as do our respective teams. There's nothing quite like a Cubs/Cards series at Wrigley Field.

And, speaking of baseball, I recall a business trip I took some years ago. Some friends and business associates of mine were sitting at an elegant bar in an upscale hotel on the east coast. It was the National Solid Waste Convention and it was the late 1960's. As I was looking around this beautiful hotel drinkery, I spotted a familiar face sitting at the end of the bar. I was relatively certain I had seen this face wearing Dodger Blue at Wrigley, but I couldn't put a name with the face. I alerted my friends and after a short discussion, we realized who it was. It was none other than the renowned Hall of Famer, retired baseball pitcher Sandy Koufax. As we discussed his historic

Dodger career, pitching as part of the one two punch of Koufax and Drysdale, we surmised he was likely the color TV commentator for tonight's Baseball game.

Koufax and Drysdale were not just Cub killers, but killers of just about every hitter who swung the lumber in the National League. Many teams have had two pitchers who produced great seasons together, but few could compare to Koufax and Drysdale in 1965. That year they compiled a 49-20 combined record with a total of 592 strikeouts and 47 complete games. Statistics like that are rare, if at all, these days. Koufax led the league with a 2.04 ERA and with Drysdale's 2.77 ERA they won the National League Pennant. The Dodgers faced the Minnesota Twins in the World Series and after 6 games the series was knotted at 3 apiece. Drysdale had pitched games 1 and 4 and was ready for game 7, but manager Walter Alston, in a move that would be unheard of today, handed the ball to Koufax on two days rest. Koufax was certainly up to the task, shutting out the Twins on only 3 hits and striking out 10, capping off the '65 season with World Series Rings for all the men in blue. Sometimes a team manager or a business owner has to think and act outside the box.

And, while we're still on the topic of baseball I'm reminded of a story my friend and business partner Tom shared with me. Tom had a baseball signed by his favorite southpaw, Braves hurler Warren Spahn. He eventually gave the ball to a friend in a men's discussion group where they shared their stories *and* their possessions. Tom had pitched in Little League and was admittedly very wild and unpredictable. He still recalls the stories he learned from the greatest game on earth. One in particular, involved the stare down between pitcher and hitter, the intensity of the way the batter looked at him and the way he looked at the batter. To Tom, moments like that expressed a great deal about many of the challenges that occur in life, a one on one battle of wits and skill. Spahn's advice still inspires all of us when it comes to making the deal. Spahn said, "What is life, after all, but a challenge? And what better challenge can there be than the one between the pitcher and the hitter." Every game we play in life, whether we win or lose, enriches us and teaches us that outcomes are shaped by our strategies and follow through.

Though it was not specifically a *business* deal in the strictest terms this chance meeting with Sandy Koufax left us all wearing smiles. You see, later that afternoon one of the Waste Management Executives appeared with a gorgeous hostess on each arm. Sandy couldn't help but notice the dazzling females and followed them with his eyes as they passed. Using baseball lingo, we traded a couple of rising up and comers for some tickets to be named later. I heard Mr. Koufax enjoyed a wonderful early dinner with the beautiful young hostesses. I know my friends and I enjoyed the evening baseball game from our complimentary front row box seats.

Sometimes life throws you a knuckleball and as Bob Uecker says, "The way to catch a knuckleball is to wait until it stops rolling and then pick it up."

The barter system, which is the purest form of business, is still alive and well. Tom reemphasized the lesson. He learned to trade baseball cards and comic books as a kid and later it was bicycles and go karts. He discovered that every place he went almost everyone had something they wanted and something they wanted to get rid of and that is the basis of a good trade. Everything is negotiable. He credits me for teaching him that when both parties walk away with smiles on their faces your faith in humanity is reaffirmed.

J. Paul Getty once reflected on the advice that his father gave: "You must never try to make all the money that's in a deal. Let the other fellow make some money too, because if you have a reputation for always making all the money, you won't have many deals." And making a deal can be almost as much fun as making money. Well, almost.

So, in the words of the late, great Harry Carey- "There she goes, way back, it might be outta here, it could be, it is A HOME RUN!"

May all your trades and all your bartering bring smiles to your faces, profits to your pockets, and advantage to everyone involved. Make every deal a win/win! In other words, home runs for both teams! As I like to say, "Quid Pro Quo" whether it's "Play Ball" for the Cubs or Otto is open for business.

Clyde likes to quote Skip the team manager from *Bull Durham*, "It's a miracle. This... is a simple game. You throw the ball. You hit the ball. You catch the ball."

Sometimes we complicate our lives unnecessarily.

There is no off season in the game of life....Batter up!

-Clyde says "Swing for the fences!"

-Hickey says "Watch out for curve balls!"

Chapter 6
Stātu Quō -
"The way it was"

It's hard to trust someone who says they are all caught up especially when paperwork is concerned. Your inbox is not supposed to be empty. So, I was *catching up* on my personal stack of papers in my Madison, Wisconsin office when an unexpected call from Waste Management Corporate Headquarters came in. I can still hear the words coming from the receiver clear and succinct. "Please attend an important meeting at 11am tomorrow!"

Clyde once shared with Tom and me how the announcement of a meeting often sparks a little anxiety in him. Just as certain childhood memories guide and define a present emotion, when a meeting is announced for later in the day, Clyde is reminded of those days as a child when his dad would say something like, "Just wait 'til we get home." This usually meant there was a price to pay for some infraction Clyde had been caught in. Having to wait until he got home was usually greater punishment than the actual punishment. So, *waiting* was torture.

As was my habit I arrived early for the meeting. Somewhat like Clyde, I was anxious to know what this "important meeting" was about. Not that I expected something bad, it was just that not knowing created a bit of anxiety. So while waiting for 11 a.m. to roll around I unsuccessfully tried to pump Rosemary for information about the reason for the meeting. She was the personal assistant to Dean Buntrock, the Corporate CEO.

The meeting started promptly at eleven and boy was I shocked and surprised. Waste Management had purchased the waste paper division of the Lissner Corporation, a large, successful and well known scrap dealer. Remember "Green" is a new term. To me and others at the time it was scrap.

My first assignment was to fly to Minneapolis to meet Ed Law a consultant hired by Waste Management to put the acquisition together. As I got off the plane, I recognized him immediately. He looked like a country bumpkin with a cigar in his mouth. Little did I know he would become my lifelong friend and a trusted mentor. Don't be fooled by appearances. Ed had an engineering degree from University of Michigan and an MBA from Harvard. He was a deadly negotiator.

After the deal was made, I was to move back to Chicago and learn the business and then become President of the new company and operate it. I was given a week to wind up things in Madison. All at once the shock and surprise turned into raw excitement. What an opportunity!!! I immediately made up my mind I would learn the new business and then turn it into the best *Waste Paper Company* in Chicago; no...in the whole Midwest. I could not wait to start. You can never give someone motivation. They have to feel it and react to it. Drive is important but passion and action is essential.

A week later I was sitting in Meyer Lissner's office, a respected waste paper executive and managing partner of the Lissner Corp, he was going to be my teacher and mentor. They moved my desk next to his and from day one I was involved in the operation of the business. It was very exciting and I learned fast. The business consisted of a processing plant and a brokerage division. The crux of the business was the brokerage operation.

Within a few months, I was buying and selling tons and tons of waste paper and developing new customers, both generators and end consumers.

It did not take long for me to realize that some of the business practices and theories that I was learning clashed with my business ideas and ethics. In the movie *Wall Street*, Gordon Gekko says, "Greed, for lack of a better word, is good." It seemed to me that we were just a bit too greedy and as I said in the previous chapter, "Quid Pro Quo". Let everybody make some money. Changes would have to be made.

What bothered me the most was the industry practice of having an adversarial business relationship between the end users, the recycling paper mills and the suppliers; the waste paper companies. In other words the mills and the waste paper companies did not trust or respect each other. Quite frankly it was "screw or be screwed."

In the industry it is described like this. When there is a shortage of waste paper the suppliers screw the mills by raising the market prices. When there is a surplus of waste paper the mills screw the waste paper companies by dropping prices and cancelling orders. I understand the principal of supply and demand, but these types of practices were going to extremes. That was not acceptable to me. I wanted a year-round business with steady orders and trust with mutual respect between the parties. I promised myself that I would change this.

Finally my training period ended, Meyer Lissner left and it was my baby. A few weeks later I noticed a change in the market conditions and a shortage of waste paper slowly developed and I decided that it was a perfect opportunity to put my plan into action. My competitors immediately started to raise prices; some stopped shipping and started selling to the highest bidders. I honored my orders and tried to help my mills by shipping more. This was a great opportunity to change the relationships with the mills. I believe in making every customer an 'A' prospect, treating them all equally. And, then when it comes to the 'bottom line', all are winners.

I worked hard to become the mills' recycling partner. Trust came slowly at first but soon mutual respect crept into the picture. As the period of waste paper shortage continued I let my competitors raise the market prices then shipped my orders faithfully and continued to develop my customer base and mill relationships. My competitors thought I was nuts. Even Ed thought I was crazy. Sometimes I began to question my decision but I stuck to it.

These market conditions lasted for almost a year then suddenly the economy took a down turn causing the waste paper shortage to become a surplus, building huge inventories at the waste paper companies. As was the custom the paper mills lowered their prices, reduced and sometimes canceled orders as a punishment for price gouging. My orders stayed the same and my pricing was reasonable. My company weathered the economic down turn with the help of my "mill recycling partners". My plan was successful and over the next few years others in the industry realized that the old adversarial relationship needed to be changed. No matter what business you're in, treat everyone like 'A' prospects. Don't think short term, but rather think of the *Big Picture*.

Tom, Clyde, and I sat at one of our watering holes in Nashville and talked about the lessons I had learned. They were simple but they must constantly be practiced:

- Never ever accept the status quo
- Always be flexible
- Always treat your customers as business *partners* and never as adversaries
- Ethics and Honesty are paramount

Clyde remarked, "So gentlemen, the way it was does not have to be the way it is."

Tom added, "Yep, the status quo is the way things were when Otto came. The *Otto quo* is the way he left them."

I guess you could say that every man or woman leaves their mark. I left mine. Leave yours.

"Shake. It's a deal. No paperwork necessary.
My word is my bond."

Chapter 7
Getting Kinky

Here we were looking for something interesting to do to kick off 2011. We wanted to give the book another fresh audience and rebrand ourselves. After meeting with Brett Darken, a sharp young filmmaker with a marketing eye at a lunch meeting at NOSHVILLE, a deli in downtown Nashville, we came to the conclusion that a new "Sheriff" was needed in town. The trend in America for some time was for "strong" men to take a backseat to the "weenie" types who never took a stand. It was time to take a stand.

It was also time to rebrand. I contacted my good friend Lennie Jones, a well known successful artist in Naples Florida, and told him we need some new photographs. Lennie's website sums up his artistic acclaim magnificently; describing himself as "a self taught primitive American Folk Artist, living in the rural Everglades Region of Southwest Florida. Lennie works primarily with acrylic paint on linen canvas, as well as occasional works on driftwood that he has discovered deep in the Everglades. Lennie's subjects generally revolve around Southern blues & roots music themes, and his creations are colorful, soulful & singularly unique. Lennie's completed works have included Festival & Event Posters, CD Covers, magazine & media, prints & portraits and he has received a wide variety of appreciative testimonials & accolades. Lennie is represented by the ACT Gallery of the beautiful Fort Myers Florida Historic District."

After Lennie agreed to do a photo shoot on the beach, we reviewed and absolutely loved the results and the new images depicted the new "me". Then came another meeting in Nashville after Brett shot a few hours of film that we hoped to use in a documentary. Tom and I sat around for hours on end thinking about who we wanted to hook up with to take our book and our ideas to a different level. We left with no clear cut path but we were convinced of one thing, we knew a lot of interesting people. We felt like Hemingway must have felt in the 1920's hanging out in Paris with creative minds like Gertrude Stein and F. Scott Fitzgerald.

Then a few days later, Tom called and said he had the answer. "It's Kinky," he screamed into the phone.

"What?" I responded.

"Kinky Friedman! We have to find away do a gig with Kinky and fine tune our new approach. Kinky is the spittin' image of a man who does things his way. A real cowboy with political ideas and a philosophy that says you can serve humankind but remain true to yourself."

Tom was right. Kinky was a man who had always done things his way. He had run for Governor of Texas in 2006, and though his campaign was colorful, it was serious nonetheless. One of his stated goals was the "dewussification" of Texas and one of his most popular slogans was "Why the Hell Not?"

We talked for the next hour about how to start and we came up with the idea of an evening of good food, adult beverages, and cigars (Kinky's own brand of course), culminating in philosophical discussion and book signings. We were extremely excited about our idea for the evening, intellect and a damn good time all rolled into one.

I knew I would have a lot in common with Kinky who once remarked that "a happy childhood... is the worst possible preparation for life." I couldn't wait to tell him about Vienna and my childhood escapades.

As I thought about our plan another quote of Kinky's came to mind. "Treat children like adults and adults like children." I guess in one's quest of creating a legacy, that message is one of the most important of all.

We contacted the living legend himself and discovered he was not only approachable but ready to come to Nashville and work together. We loved him and his capitalistic side. We set a date in January and had a Kinky poster made with Tom and I sitting on a Harley with cigars, looking like the metaphorical cowboys we had chosen to be.

We called our old running buddy and Clyde stepped in to do his normal P.R. job and we teamed up with The Smokey Cigar, a local business and beautiful venue for an event like we had in mind.

In between my arrival in Nashville and Kinky's, we hooked up with some young filmmakers to do a trailer for another movie idea, an Orwellian type independent film about my experiences set in the future. We might as well, we thought. There are a lot of ideas out there and you got to keep trying new things.

The day of the event had us running to the airport and snatching Kinky and his longtime sidekick, Little Jewford. On our way,

Tom and I mused about how our first meeting would be. It turned out much better than we expected as we bonded immediately with the Kinkster. He invited us to appear with him at his next show in Nashville, which would give us the podium to once again share my story and promote our book. We blushed but were honored when a great lover of literature like Kinky said our book was one of his favorite reads of the year.

On the way to breakfast we passed the building that housed Manuel Cuevas' show room and workshop. Manuel is a famed fashion designer for Rock and Roll, Hollywood and Country & Western stars. Cuevas created Johnny Cash's black suits and crafted Elvis' signature gold lamé suit, and even designed wardrobe for Roy Rogers and the Lone Ranger early in his career.

I recalled how Manuel graciously lent me a fabulous Blue Sequined Jacket to wear to a fund raiser for Otto Productions held at Vernon Winfrey, father of Oprah, and his wife's home. Actor David Keith stopped by for the event. Earlier we met David and listened as he described his passion for **Promise to Protect**, a national organization dedicated to the protection of children from abuse and neglect. Clyde, Tom, and I have enjoyed his work over the years in such roles as Larry Lee Bullen in the film *Brubaker*, starring Robert Redford, and Elvis Presley in *Heartbreak Hotel*, in addition to his most notable role as Richard Gere's buddy, Sid Whorley, in *An Officer and a Gentleman*. He is a man full of passion and talent. I keep meeting new people who have what it takes. Yep, Nashville has been good to me over the years.

We delivered Kinky to the Hyatt Place in Hendersonville, TN where our buddy Clyde conducted an interview with Friedman on topics ranging from football to politics, while we sat thoroughly entertained as Kinky expounded for an hour and a half. As we were being enlightened by the Kinkster in this hotel conference room, the skies opened up and dumped a couple of inches of that heavenly white stuff we know as snow all over middle Tennessee. If you have ever been driving the roads in Nashville in the middle of a snowstorm, it isn't pretty or "purty", as Clyde would say. But despite the road conditions left by this concentrated freezing of water vapor in the air, we had a great turnout. Folks came all the way from Birmingham, and as far away as Boston and Baltimore.

My trip was capped off with a dash back to the Washington area, where I had been invited to attend an event hosted by the Ambassador from Morocco. It was a very exciting evening and I was honored to present him with a copy of our book, *Otto, the Boy at the Window*.

Tom and I had agreed to get together again in May and we did. We spent another nice evening with Kinky at 3rd and Lindsley, a swinging hotspot as Tom calls it, in Nashville signing more books and listening to great music with friends before ending up at Margaritaville for a nightcap.

Tom often talks of a little theatre where he sang Alice's Restaurant and he repeats the words sometimes to Clyde and me to make a point about why we do what we do. He gets emotional sometimes. He says he is a passionate man. Clyde and I don't dispute that. We know he loves us and we love him and isn't that alone something special? After all as I often say, Love rules. So we indulge his rants. I can hear him now....

We want to say to everyone no matter where you come from or what you've been through, everything's gonna be alright. Yep, that's a righteous movement, one that decrees that life is okay. Sing a bar of your favorite Kinky song and rebrand yourself. It works and as Kinky might say *"Why the hell not?"*

"Smile boys! Oh, why the hell not?
Let's just have some fun."

Chapter 8
Phones Planes and Automobiles

Every now and then when I am using my cell phone, my thoughts go back to my first mobile phone, though it wasn't really that mobile at all. Actually, they just called them car phones in those days. You get the picture. Anyway, it was the mid sixties and I was in charge of business development in the state of Wisconsin. I had been pestering my boss for one of those new fangled phones for a long time. One day a box arrived from the phone company and I was very excited as I opened the box and found a black dial phone like folks had in their homes.

The dealer sent an installer and he wired the phone and attached it to the floor of the car by the front seat. In order to make a call you had to give the mobile operator the number you wanted. Sometimes it took as long as twenty minutes to reach the mobile operator. My buddy Clyde didn't get his first mobile phone until the mid eighties and it was considered the portable kind. It came in a container about the size of a lunch box, and could be used anywhere as long as the 6 lb. battery was charged. The meaning of the word 'mobile' has certainly changed, hasn't it?

I was very proud of my new phone and started using it immediately. A few days later I had just dropped my son off at school, and a call came in from one of our company suppliers. We got into a heated discussion about a pending purchase order. While I was busy yelling on the phone, I went through a stop sign and smashed into another car. Both cars were totaled. The only thing still working on the car was the dial tone from my new mobile phone. Distracted driving is nothing new and is as dangerous today as it was then. The advice on this matter is simple. Don't do it.

Tom and I were cruising in his Corvette in Lexington, Kentucky after visiting with a client and as we emerged from the Marriott Hotel, a concrete truck ran the traffic light and we swerved sideways. We both could feel the air from the big truck as it roared past and went into the median at a high rate of speed, only clearing us by inches. We were doing nothing wrong and though we believe in fate, we also believe in science. So do anything you can do to beat the odds. You just never know what might happen!

We all know that air travel today, even at its best, is a pain in the neck. In the sixties, it was easy and a lot of fun. My company instituted a program for the managers that consisted of a book of tickets and all you had to do was present it at the check-in counter. The ticket agent would tear out a ticket and give you a boarding pass. They would then bill the company at the end of the month. It did not take me long to figure out that those tickets also worked in first class. Here is a piece of advice for everyone. When you can, go first class. You meet people who can help you in many ways. Contacts are "everything" in business.

In those days you were allowed to smoke on planes and you could even smoke cigars in first class. Imagine a nice cigar, a superb glass of wine and a nice conversation with a worldly traveler in the window seat. Those were the glory days of travel.

Yes, I remember one day I was sitting in first class enjoying one of my favorite stogies when a lady sitting a few rows back started to complain that my cigar was making her sick. I should have just told her that you're not supposed to inhale, but I doubt she would have gotten the point. The stewardess was really sweet and asked me politely to put out my cigar. Everyone needed to enjoy the trip and since she probably *paid* for her ticket, I was glad to oblige. I put out the cigar and chewed on it the rest of the trip. As payment for snuffing out my flavorful stogie, I was rewarded with a refill of fine brandy. When the plane landed I waited for the folks behind me to get off first. As the complaining lady with a big frown passed by my seat I dropped the freshly chewed butt into her purse. Call it "poetic justice", if you will or just a little "road warrior" fun. Anyway, sorry lady wherever you are.

Tom is a million-miler on several airlines and Clyde has lived all around the country including the West Coast. Clyde once asked his dad what you call a man who has spent very little time in one place (referring to himself), and his dad replied, "a drifter". So, traveling is the way a Businessman and a Renaissance man …and even a drifter, gets seasoned.

The old sage Seneca thought "Travel and change of place impart new vigor to the mind." The things I have seen and the places I have gone and the people I've met have added vigor to my mind. They tell us a great deal about this world and the lives we lead are reflective of where we've been.

Hit the gas and hold on! Or as Clyde says when he's teeing up "Grip it and rip, boys!*"

*With all respect to Golf Legend Mr. Loudmouth himself, John Daly

Chapter 9
Groveling 101

The dictionary defines groveling quite simply: <u>to humble oneself or act in an abject manner.</u> To me, groveling is a mere skirmish in the war of business designed to keep your customer happy and to make them feel guilty that they questioned your loyalty. In the analysis of Sun Tzu, "Humble words and increased preparations are signs that the enemy is about to advance. Violent language and driving forward as if to the attack are signs that he will retreat." He finishes with this thought, 'To begin by bluster, but afterwards to take fright ... shows a supreme lack of intelligence."

Hickey and I were on our way to Boston to deal with an equipment problem at one of our better customers. When we arrived, we found it fairly easy to size up the situation. The equipment was marginal, probably a little too small for the job. The customer had convinced himself that it would not do the job. In other words they wanted it out of there. Tom and I knew the problems were partly their fault and partly the fault of the manufacturer. We certainly didn't want to lose this customer. It was *Groveling Time*. I told them we would take back the equipment, at no cost to them, and install a different piece of equipment more suitable for their needs.

On the way home we realized we would have to convince the manufacturer to take back the equipment and pay the freight in and out if we were to break even. I volunteered to handle the problem. Back at the office I got on the phone and had a mini-tantrum, a strategy that works with certain personality types, and began telling them their equipment was not right for the job and that I had promised the customer we would take it back at no cost to them. I remember telling them we were in jeopardy of losing the customer. Tom was certainly privy to the call and reminded me later that I also told them if they did not work with us I would jump off the nearest bridge. Clyde and Tom are the actors but I am also quite a thespian myself. Well, the actor in me paid off and after a long discussion they agreed to take back the equipment *and* pay the freight.

Though it is not specific to this point, I am reminded of a short story Clyde shared with me about a distribution company he worked for back in the early eighties. He was having a particular delivery challenge with one of his customers, primarily because his customer was having a challenge of his own staying current on his bill. So Clyde decided to have a sit down with the distribution manager. This was in Northern California, but Jerry, the distribution manager, was originally from East Tennessee and was known for some pretty colorful phrases. Being in any kind of business where shipping is involved, the terms C.O.D. (cash on delivery) and F.O.B. (freight on board) are pretty common. When Clyde pressed Jerry for a solution, Jerry simply responded with, "CODFOB". Unclear as to why the distribution manager would run these two phrases together, Clyde respectfully asked for an explanation to which Jerry responded, "Cash on Delivery or Fetchit' on Back." Jerry moved back to East Tennessee some time later and left this world just a few short years ago when cancer reared its ugly head. Tom and I would have liked to have met Jerry but are fortunate to have made his acquaintance, so to speak, through our buddy Clyde. We certainly liked his collection technique.

Well, the end of my story is like this. We saved our relationship with the customer and didn't take a bath on the project. And as far as the manufacturer was concerned, we bought more the next year than the previous five combined. That's the way it sometimes goes.

When I stood on the stage with Clyde and young Thomas Kohann, two actors who portrayed me in various stages of my life, I was reminded that role playing is essential in the world of entertainment *and* in the world of business. As I joined the cast and took my bow at curtain call, I felt the synergy of people working together. I also knew that only hours before, we had lighting problems and sound problems and the chance that our play's premiere would be a flop. Tom remained calm and said there is magic when it comes to opening night of a show and somehow it would come together. Not coming from the world of theatre, I was not so confident and saw hours and hours of hard work and lots of money going down the drain. I had people coming to Nashville to see the play from all areas of the country. I was more than a little concerned. But as showtime got closer, things began to work out. We begged the tech people to make it happen even when they said it might not. Led by Tom's example, we kept a positive attitude though our guts were wrenching. Courage is indeed "grace under pressure". Anxiously, we watched as the curtain went up, not knowing quite what to expect. As the curtain fell on the final act, I finally breathed the infamous sigh of relief. For not only were our expectations exceedingly met, the show was spectacular! I stood backstage about to take my very first curtain call bow ever with two of the people who made it all possible. Tom and writer/director William Dorian were not only applauding the show but also the fact that we had pulled it off. I am reminded that there is a Higher Power at work.

We have walked cold turkey into book stores and other organizations and pitched our books and offered to come back anytime to do a presentation. We love the chance to look a manager or an owner in the eye and make our pitch. Rarely do we fail to get an opportunity of some kind because "groveling" with passion says to an individual or a group, we mean business and we care about our product, be it a piece of equipment or a book that tells the story of Otto, the boy at the window who became the man at the wheel. Groveling and aggression like love and hate are very much alike. It's important to know the subtle differences.

Live hard. Play hard. Then graciously take your bow!

Chapter 10
Glue Buddies and the Beauty of Smiling

Let's face it. When you are dealing with flesh and blood human beings, you have problems. The world of recycling is no different, but perhaps a little more interesting. Tom had acquired a project in Anaheim, California in the late 80's and we had used our usual crew from Memphis who had contracted with some labor from the local area. As is sometimes the case, things went awry. There were delays, and since Tom was in another region of the country, I hopped on a jet and made my way to Southern California. It brought back memories of when I had lived in the area back in the late fifties.

On my way out there, I thought about the fact that technology never replaces a personal face to face meeting. I still live by that principle. You should always be willing to suck it up and get in a car or on a train or a jet and make a bee line for the source of your problems. You have to believe that no one can do it like you. No one can.

It was a mess. I told the guy I met there was a new plan. I was staying there until this thing was finished and we got paid. He was going to see me every day. We were going to be, in his vernacular, "glue buddies". So I stuck with him until things were on track, until the thing was finished, and until we got paid.

Some people are easily motivated and can get things done on their own. Others need a glue buddy. They may not like it but until they can ride their bike without training wheels, someone needs to prop them up, sit them straight on the seat, square their shoulders and give the command. "Pedal!"

I've told Tom since we first started working together that the hours invested in a project were not as important as the result. Entrepreneurs are like that. They work hard. They achieve results. But they also play hard because they consider their time off an opportunity to recharge the batteries and get a fresh perspective. You can't fight beyond your strength no matter how hard you try. The day that you can finally free a glue buddy from having a babysitter is the greatest moment of their careers. For the first time perhaps, they are ready to do it entirely on their own. It doesn't mean they don't ask for or need help from time to time but at the core they believe they can do it. A good mentor watches from the distance and loves being a teacher always cautioning the student that change can instill fear. Be prepared to help the people around you conquer their fear.

Now the ancient Jewish teachers have said "Don't open a shop unless you know how to smile." It is important to be confident I always tell Clyde and Hickey but it is also important to smile. That is the first thing I notice when I see Clyde, he is always smiling and he always has a piece of good news to deliver about this and that. Clyde says an acting coach of his once told him that when you walk into an audition you should be thinking to yourself, "I am beautiful, I am loved, and I have a secret." Feeling beautiful gives you confidence, being loved evokes security, and having a secret gives you a sense of mystery. Maybe Clyde's smile is because he has a secret.

A good sense of humor and a quick wit can get you through the most difficult of circumstances. On one particular occasion Tom was in a meeting about some noisy equipment he installed at a plant that was causing the cows at a dairy farm, located next door, to produce less milk than normal, according to the owner. After some discussion about noise levels the conversation got quite heated. Tom stood up and said "This meeting is an *udder* disaster." Silence fell on the room. But Tom was committed to making his point so he stood there simulating with his hands the motions a dairy farmer makes when milking a cow. He continued "milking the cow" until everyone got the message and finally when the uncomfortable feeling wore off, the room broke into laughter. Tom certainly knows how to make a point. After the laughter stopped, someone said perhaps we can work something out and split the costs. We did.

On another occasion in L.A., we were at a restaurant having a lively discussion with our rep from Portland. We were supposed to be quiet because the servers sang opera arias, as part of their gimmick. We were not the most gracious patrons as we were loud and perhaps a little inebriated. Suddenly there was a pause in the middle of Figaro's aria. We were all projecting at a level as loud as the performer and were likely even more dramatic. Tom is very charismatic and with the emphasis of his big hand gestures, the whole restaurant knew our business. As you might imagine, we were asked to leave. In retrospect I think we should have taken a bow. Needless to say, our departure seemed most gratifying to the other serious theatre type patrons. We all got a big laugh out of the affair as we made our way back to the hotel forming a bond with our rep that would not be forgotten. A little larceny goes a long way.

When Tom, Clyde, or I have a public speaking engagement, we don't really use a script. We prefer to just throw out a general concept and "run with it". It comes across more natural and we have all found that speaking from the heart in an impromptu manner is more sincere and allows a greater interaction with the audience. So in effect, we are smiling "glue buddies" there to present the Otto message and also to demonstrate the lesson of friends working together toward a common goal.

That model works in business and in life and I hope that you always remember the words of wisdom from the old clever ones of times past- "The only truly dead are those who have been forgotten." Clyde says it's the actor's responsibility to listen *and* to be heard. So I say, be heard. And, make yourself *unforgettable*. We are doing our best and smiling every minute as we do it.

"Here's the deal. Be remarkable and be it now!"

Chapter 11
California Scheming and Learning from the SEALs

California was a great place to live. It was so great I decided to live there twice. I spent my winters there for a while. I got my dose of inspiration in those days in the late 1980's and early 1990's getting up early and enjoying the best climate in the States. It was a cool place to take a stroll and head past the main beach area and see the start of a boardwalk behind the Hotel Del Coronado. It ran for about three-quarters of a mile behind the hotel. It reminded me of Billy Wilder's classic film made there, *Some Like It Hot*. At low tide you could catch a glimpse of the Monte Carlo, a sunken gambling ship that washed ashore in 1936. What gave me the greatest inspiration was watching the Navy SEALs running along the beach, especially as you head south towards the Silver Strand. Coronado is where they train.

Whenever I think of guts and self confidence, I am always reminded of the Navy SEALs. These guys certainly have an ample supply of both. These warriors are a highly trained breed of the U.S. Navy's principal special operations force and a part of the Naval Special Warfare Command as well as the maritime component of the United States Special Operations Command. SEAL is an acronym derived from their capacity to operate at sea, in the air, and on land. They are members of either the United States Navy or the United States Coast Guard, with special consideration also given to Marine Corps, Army, and Air Force Special Operatives for the purpose of cross training. Perhaps the movie *G.I. Jane* was a bit of an embellishment.

SEAL training is brutal and considered the toughest training anywhere in the world. Their drop-out rate is about 80 percent. The average Navy SEAL spends over a year in a series of formal training environments. Upon graduation they are awarded the Special Warfare Operator Naval Rating and the Navy Enlisted Classification 5326 Combatant Swimmer (SEAL). One of my favorite sayings I've heard attributed to the SEALs is:

"To find us, you must be good...To catch us, you must be quick...To defeat us; you must be joking!"

Staying one step ahead of the game is a key in business and frankly most other things in life. Another Navy SEAL's saying is "The only easy day was yesterday." As I reflect on the things that happened to me, let me make something perfectly clear, I didn't know I was learning lessons that I would one day write about. I was trying to cover my ass and work through my problems and earn enough dough to pay my bills. We all have that in common. But later on, when the smoke has cleared it is time to reflect and learn and "tweak" as Tom says.

We worked very hard coming up with plans for a major trading card company. We gave them a lot of information and made many visits only to have the deal pulled at the last minute and given to someone else. It was a crushing blow but in the end you eventually learn, usually after being screwed a few times, to give as much information as you have to and nothing more. There comes a time when the "free lunch" stops. Some jobs turned out to be simply consultation services and for that we began to get paid. And you learn that some deals require that you say "No" and walk away and count the money you didn't lose rather than the money you might have made.

Sometimes a small businessman goes bankrupt. Some ideas just don't translate into moneymakers. Tom had to bite the bullet when he found out he couldn't be on the road 300 days a year and run a manufacturing facility.

Both of us have made bad real estate investments and when they go sour, you just have to take your lumps. Tom's business foray into the cigar craze was exciting but market conditions shifted quickly and government regulations saw his business plan bite the dust and, pardon the pun, ended up in *ashes*. He almost cried at the time but now laughs about it as "just another one of those things that didn't work out". Henry Ward Beecher said, "One's best success comes after their greatest disappointments. That reminds me of a Napoleon Hill quote. He said, "Every adversity, every failure, every heartache carries with it the seed on an equal or greater benefit."
It is no crime to fall down. It is a crime not to get up.

We have a patent for a static control system that worked well but for some reason from a marketing perspective just didn't take off. As Tom says, "You know, Pete, most people who invent something never get it patented. At least, we gave it the old college try." He's right. Our failures define our successes.

Clyde often talks about the life of an actor. He says every actor knows that despite a great audition, you don't always get the role or even a "call back". Perhaps you don't look the part, maybe you're too young or too old, or maybe it's just not your turn. The bottom line is, you can't brood about it or overanalyze it. The only way to overcome losing a part you wanted is to just move on. There may have been 50 guys auditioning for that one part. Statistics are not in your favor, so chalk it up to another lesson learned, and go get the next one. Get your butt in gear!

We have all learned to move on if we are to grow and we see our whole life in terms of small chunks of it. Sometimes we hold our breath and live by faith and hope that what we are doing is the right thing. Sometimes it is. Sometimes it is not. But in a greater sense it has always been like that. I take great comfort when I refer to the words of the mystic Shem Tov ibn Shem Tov, "How did God create the world? Like a person taking a deep breath and holding it, so that the small contains the large." I hope my small tales paint a larger picture of a life well lived.

Life's a real beach!
And sometimes a real bitch.
Hickey says he's been called both.
Clyde agrees.

Chapter 12
Vita mutatur, non tollitur -
(Life is changed, not taken away)

Publius Vergilius Maro or as we know him, Virgil, travelled with Augustus to Greece. There, he caught a fever, from which he died leaving the *Aeneid* unfinished. Augustus ordered Virgil's literary executors to disregard Virgil's own wish that the poem be burned, instead ordering it published with as few changes as possible.

Another example I might add of the practicalities of politics overriding the romance of art and literature. My politics are simple. Private matters are none of the government's business and other than protecting me from enemies, foreign and domestic, and providing roads and other similar services, the government has one main role and that is to promote business so that people who work hard have a shot at the American Dream, the dream I believed in and got me where I am today.

As a result of ignoring Virgil's request, the text of the *Aeneid* that exists may contain faults which Virgil was planning to correct before he shared the story with the world. Who really cares you might say? Well that's the gist of my lesson. He cared and it was his property to do with what he pleased, even burning it if he wanted.

Incomplete or not, whether Virgil liked it or not, the *Aeneid* was immediately recognized as a masterpiece and still is today. Sure it proclaimed the imperial mission of the Roman Empire, but at the same time could pity Rome's victims and feel their grief.

The hero Aeneas struggles between doing what he wants to do as a man, and doing what he must as a virtuous hero. I can attest to the fact that doing both is quite a task. But to be successful you must.

Tom thinks that the real lesson here is that to be a real human being is to repeat patterns. Some are more trying than others, of course. The issue is not the pattern, but the interior pattern-maker within ourselves who loves to tell us what our pain means based on our past experience with it. Look. Dealing with Nazis was no picnic for a young kid. Dealing with school bullies in my Chicago neighborhood was no walk in the park. Dealing with jerks in the business world wasn't much fun either. But my past experiences like Clyde's, Tom's and yours teach us a lot about our present attitude as I have alluded to earlier.

I have established at least a couple of patterns based upon two pieces of sound advice from Virgil that I use every day: *Love conquers all* & *Mind moves matter*. When my wife Bonnie, my children, and my grandchildren call me Otto, it reminds me that any pain I have suffered has been a small price to pay to have a family like mine. And the decision we make in our own minds to succeed makes things happen especially when a lot of elbow grease is also applied.

My beliefs are in part connected to Greek and Roman thought as well as Jewish tradition.

It now appears from what I can glean that my solution presented was remarkably similar to that applied by Virgil to the problems and challenges of Augustan society. And in this case, imitation is not just *a sincere form of flattery so much as a profound expression of competition.* As I am also a capitalist, competition in my view is a good thing that creates a thriving economy and as a free thinker, the freedom to compete means that the best ideas and ideals will spring forth.

One day, I strolled away from a corporate meeting in the Northeast after our largest account was lost as a part of a merger. Imagine that! My son-in-law, Lloyd and my long time friend, Irwin and I made our way toward the rental car. After joking about who had enough money to buy lunch, I came to the conclusion that we were going to have to make more out of less. Lloyd went on to replace the large account with many smaller accounts each having less of an impact if we lost one. By taking this approach, we protected ourselves against this type of setback again. Nietzsche said, "That which does not kill us makes us stronger." And, to that I would add Virgil's advice that life is changed not taken away.

Otto would say, at least not for now and now is all we've got.

When in doubt, THINK!

Clyde says- "When you got it figured out.
Stop thinkin'."
Hickey says- "Then start drinkin'."

Chapter 13
One Thing Leads to Another

Tom and Clyde are always talking about the fact that you start out in one direction and you end up taking all these little detours that make the journey even more exciting than you could have imagined. In the movie, *Mr. Destiny*, the lead character Larry Burrows is given a rare opportunity to relive his life beginning with a single swing of a bat in a baseball game he played in high school. By striking out instead of hitting that pitch, which turned out to be the last pitch of the game, he believed that his life had been destined to one of mediocrity as opposed to something great. Through a chance meeting with an otherworldly character, Larry was afforded a real life glimpse into the life he would have lived had he hit that pitch. In the end, he learned that missing that pitch led to meeting the true love of his life, Ellen. Though it was not by choice to miss that pitch, Burrows learned that something as insignificant as hitting or missing a pitch could dramatically alter the entire course of your life. So, set you intentions on doing the right thing and know that each morning affords us with the prospect of something new. And remember if you can't improve something at the very least, preserve it.

It all started with an e-mail from a good friend in Nashville: *Spoke with Ron Browning, a critically acclaimed Voice Coach and an accomplished Jazz Pianist, he mentioned Dietlinde Turbon Maazel, one of his students who is an actress of note and the wife of the famous Maestro Loren Maazel Director of the New York Philharmonic. Ron felt Dietlinde would be perfect as Karla, my mother, in our play "OTTO". He promised to contact her.*

A few weeks later our friend, Lynda called and told us that Ron had heard from Dietlinde. She had read our book and play. She loved the general storyline and told us she would like to come to Nashville for a meeting.

So we set it up and exchanged our ideas. Over dinner, Tom suggested a Black Box Production with Dietlinde playing Karla, my mother. It seemed a perfect fit. The meeting couldn't have been better and after exchanging life stories with Dietlinde, I felt a bond of friendship forming with this beautiful and remarkable lady.

Tom, Clyde, and I have teleconferences and face to face meetings every week or two about how to massage the ideas we have together and apart. I was thinking the other morning about the old Hebrew saying that goes something like this- "Dream as if you'll live forever, live as if you'll die today". Or was that James Dean?

Anyhow, as we each pursued our individual dreams, I continued to exchange e-mails with Dietlinde. Then one day Tom and I received an invitation to visit Castleton Farms. The Farm, situated on 108 acres of rolling hillside with lovely mountain views culminating in the Manor which offers four beautifully decorated guest rooms, two parlors and the family great room, all of which is at the disposal of guests.

Scattered about the property you can find pavilions, sculptures and flowers, and exotic animals which emit a feeling of grandeur that all Castleton's guests enjoy. The gardens are lit at night with white party lights that make it feel as if you are dancing amongst the stars. It was a wonderful experience.

We were treated to a performance of soprano Sylvia McNair, accompanied by Ted Taylor at the piano. A short time later I received an invitation from the Ambassador of His Majesty the King of Morocco to attend a Dinner to celebrate the third birthday of the Castleton Festival with guests of honor Maestro Lorin Maazel and Mrs. Dietlinde Turban Maazel. I continue to follow their remarkable lives. We don't know where this will lead, perhaps nowhere, but we will always remember and like any good salesman follow a "good lead".

Clyde has been a champion of the arts and we all feel that music and theatre as well as our passion for literature has expanded our lives and made us all better businessmen. We all speak of a new Renaissance when the higher aspirations of humankind will lead us to new places where technology is a tool for the noble calling we all feel inside.

The moral of this story is about following every opportunity and allowing your relationships the chance to grow and mature. And as usual, there is a distinction between merely saying you have a dream and actually doing something about it. As the Old Italian sages used to declare, "Many a pair of shoes is worn out between saying and doing."

Lights. Camera. Action.

Clyde quotes Steve McQueen "When I believe in
something, I fight like hell for it."
Hickey thinks, "Money talks, Bullshit walks."

Chapter 14
Classic Americans

Tom often quotes Plato who said that *Love is a serious mental disease.* I guess Tom, Clyde and I are self proclaimed nut jobs because we all love life and are constantly inventing ways to enjoy it more. Tom streaked in college and Clyde likes the Cardinals but I won't hold that against them. I once got in the book depository at the library in Chicago and tossed books back out the "in" slot at surprised ladies. Sort of sounds like an episode from *Candid Camera.* I guess not all ideas are good ones. But seriously, you never know unless you try.

Inventing is a combination of brains and materials. Clyde quotes, "Take the obvious, add a cupful of brains, a generous pinch of imagination, a bucketful of courage and daring, stir well and bring to a boil."

John Steinbeck had such an insight into America in some of its most significant years. He said *ideas are like rabbits. You get a couple and learn how to handle them, and pretty soon you have a dozen.*

Tom once told me about the first time he read *Think and Grow Rich.* He retained a phrase that I think about most every day. *Thoughts are Things.* Hill expounds, Yep, most every*thing* starts out as a *thought* that somebody has. Hill states so eloquently, "Thoughts mixed with definiteness of purpose, persistence, and a burning desire are powerful things."

The concept of the light bulb representing an idea is quite cool but in the end I side with Rabbi Harold Kushner who says that perhaps *we are here to change the world with small acts of thoughtfulness done daily rather than with one great breakthrough.*

Love may indeed be crazy in that when it is most real we are out of our minds and into our soul. Ideas are so light because they are "hazy wave states" of reality instead of solid objects that are touched.

Chesterton remarked that the reason angels can fly is that they take themselves so lightly. I say the reason humans can dream is because they see things not only as they are, but as they can be.

Speaking of men with vision, earlier I spoke of Brett Darken. When Tom and I first met Brett, we liked him immediately. He is one of those exceptional people who is at the same time humble but possesses an aura of self confidence. We spent an afternoon with him at the Gerst Haus in Nashville, a local establishment since 1955 that serves a really good schooner of dark beer, talking about our ideas and his in the tradition of civilized gentlemen.

Brett was a good listener but not afraid to voice his opinion. I was astonished, when recently, after a short telephone conversation with him; I was privileged to receive the following beautiful and touching e-mail.

Dear Peter and Tom:

You guys reflect the best of America. Hard working, creative, fun, imperfect, patient, passionate, caring and kind.

I love the immigrant optimism that still comes out of your spirit, and your willingness to accept the good times with the bad. In doing this, you allow others to learn from your successes AND your mistakes.

At work, or at play, you are guys that are fun to be with. You have a great respect for fair play, while not letting the rules get in the way of success.

I like the work-hard/play-hard spirit that you bring to your days---and because you make work fun, going the extra mile is easy to do!

You are a classic American!

Love to you both

Brett Darken
North Star Films

Some of the images Brett captured on film for us have allowed us to explore a deeper more human side of the events that shaped my life. I shall be eternally grateful for that.
How honored I felt to be called a "classic American" by a man who himself could bear that title and wear it well.

Yes, I am a Holocaust survivor who escaped Nazi occupied Vienna Austria over 70 years ago through the courage of a father with the support of some fine Americans. I became a successful entrepreneur because of the pro-business milieu in this great land. What comes to my mind when thinking about the phrase "classic American" are the virtues that instilled me to never stop dreaming, to pursue my goals, to learn from my mistakes, to respect others and most of all to adopt an attitude that proclaimed-NO WHINING. When I served in the Air Force of my new country, I did my job and expected no thanks. I learned to take orders. This also applies to the world of business especially when taking purchase orders. You must learn to take instructions in order to learn to give them.

"Serve...but expect no thanks."

"If a man does his best, what else is there?"
- General George Patton Jr.

Chapter 15
Renaissance Men

"I once half assed a pitching wedge off the tee of a short par three right into the cup", said Clyde. "I guess half assed ain't half bad sometimes." I guess not.

And, by doing so, you can do a lot of things fairly well without being an expert and you will never be boring because of your diversity. Take golf for instance, one hole I might par or on very rare occasions birdie and on the next hole, I might duck hook one and take the shingles off the side of the house that someone is brave enough to build on the edge of a fairway. I still love it though it's not for everyone.

Kinky Friedman says, "I don't like golf. The only good ball I ever hit was when I stepped on a rake."

I'm not exactly a polymath, a word derived from the Greeks meaning "understanding or having learnt in quantity", but perhaps, I am a little Leonardo DaVinci-esque or simply a person who excels in multiple fields, particularly in both the arts and sciences while making a business deal. You can be very philosophical when you have cash in your pocket.

Now Tom has fallen off many skateboards and surfboards, much to his body's chagrin. Tony Hawk has nothing to fear from Hickey and he will not be cast in the next film version of Endless Summer. But he loves the fun of doing it even if it takes a bottle of Advil to keep doing it.

The common term for this phenomenon today is Renaissance man, but also one could be called a Homo universalis or Uomo universale, both of which translate as "universal person" or "universal man" depending on your Greek or Latin leanings. I am not Will Durant when it comes to philosophy, but I love to read and study men and women who take the time to think and I have my moments in between being a bonehead, when I see the wisdom in all things.

Jack of all Trades, master of none is a common figure of speech, describing a person who is competent with many skills but is not very good with any one particular skill. The term has become as Wikipedia notes a bit cliché, but I hear it all the time. Actually the Jack of all Trades term is a truncated version of the true epithet. The figure of speech in its entirety is "Jack of all trades, master of none, though ofttimes better than master of one". I like that.

The term *Jill of all trades* is gaining usage to describe women who are similarly skilled. It's about time. I am a believer that if it works for me it works for everybody. Your personal life is none of my business unless you ask me to get involved. Meanwhile I will love you and if given the opportunity will try to make a deal with you. Now that's fun.

My favorite term for half-assed is *Johannes factotum* ("Johnny do-it-all") now that I have discovered it. Famously, the term was used by Robert Greene in the earliest surviving written reference to Shakespeare. Greene disparages Shakespeare (under the name 'Shake-scene') for being an actor who has the temerity to write plays, and for committing out and out plagiarism.

I have plagiarized in a way having borrowed some of what I know and do from a lot of you, my many friends who read this book. I have observed and learned from your work ethics, the way you treat people and your zest for life and adopted it for my own. Isn't that the greatest form of flattery or something like that?

Most of all I have taken the reflection of all that is good that I see in each of you and incorporated it with my individual experience. Anyone who knows Clyde, Tom, or me also know that we always have a list of things we want to try and places we want to go coupled with a desire to meet and see and interact with interesting people. I learned to realize that it is much easier to love than to criticize. Try it. After all there is no shortage of critics in the world.

Therefore for today, I dub myself, *Otto Factotum*, Otto do-it-all. I'm going to give it a go. Time is running out for us all. Make the best of it.

Friendship requires guts! Guts require friendship!

Chapter 16
Shifting Gears

I often think of myself as you've seen as Otto at the wheel of my vehicles but also at the wheel steering my way through life. Automatics are fine, but I like shifting gears sometimes manually and double clutching is not out of the question; multi-tasking as you go along your merry way.

Remember the phrase, Murphy's Law? Well, one of those *if it can go wrong it will* days happened recently. So I thought I would just think about something more lighthearted in nature. Like the questions of absolute truth that have been raised over the years. To what degree do philosophies of truth avoid paradox?

Tom calls that situation *the consistency of inconsistency.*

Can assertions about the future be true *now*? Can the term "is true" be completely defined or is it like Jack Nicholson stating defiantly in *A Few Good Men*, "you can't handle the truth!" I might add even if we really knew what it was.

Yeah, this I know is a diversionary tactic from "real" problems. Point taken. But hear me out. I like satire and old sayings from different cultures. I say all of this to say that we are not the first ones to have to deal with this stuff.

For instance, the Arabs would say something like: "Put your faith in Allah, but tie up your camel." We Jews and Christians use a similar saying like "God helps those who help themselves." Once I realized that the old *I* was a new *me*, somewhere on that boat that brought me from Europe to America for the first time, my first wish was for a little truth in my life. The Nazis lied. All the people who said they were good neighbors lied. My own government lied. I determined that a man's a man who looks a man right between the eyes and at least makes an attempt at truthfulness. On acting, James Cagney said, "Find your mark, look the other fellow in the eye, and tell the truth." Sounds like a good practice for everyday living.

That was realized for me after that epiphany and that remains unchanged for me today. I consider there is a level of things and people that may not ever be fully understood by me. I'm okay with that part. I had to be eager and willing to make the journey to a new and strange place and live beyond a subjective truth I had always been told about and in this new place most of us call reality. In poker, it's called playing with the hand you've been dealt. Are you in or are you out?

To that end, those days when shit happens and everything seems to go wrong I look out the window as I've always done. That helps me get a clear perspective. Then I know that those days exist in my short term state of emotional truth called being "pissed off" without being "really" true at all. I know that is purely conjecture on my part and I still grind the gears when I shift every now and then especially on steep grades.

Tom and I are both big believers in taking a walk and blowing off a little steam. Tom talks about this a lot and says that most of us walk 1-2 miles per day or more than 30,000 miles during our natural life. Two-thirds of us say our feet hurt from time to time. Over half say it's normal for their feet to hurt all the time. Madison Avenue may lure you into cramming your feet into shoes that just don't fit right causing defects and discomfort such as blisters and ingrown toenails, for starters.

Take off your shoes and save money. Get some sun on those dogs and get rid of those corns and calluses. Go outside and get them good and dirty. Your leg muscles will become toned and your gait will look youthful. Believe me if you go barefoot, you will definitely look before you leap.

And if you are lucky and work hard and have a fine wife like Bonnie, you just might end up in a paradise like Naples, Florida. And just like me, you can watch the sunset over the gulf and put your life in overdrive.

Use the clutch, Sucker!

Clyde adds "Grind it 'til you find it!"

Hickey calls out "Shotgun!"

Chapter 17
Busted

There are times in everyone's life when you get *busted* for this that or the other. You step over the line a little bit. You get a little too cocky. Tom tells me his Mom called it "getting' a little too big for your britches."

It was a tumultuous time and the Korean War was starting to heat up. I had finished High School and starting College. Young men my age were getting drafted, trained quickly and shipped overseas. Clyde's dad was in the Navy and served on a demining ship. Their job was to clear the way for the rest.

During a weak moment, maybe because I wanted to escape my Mother, I made that rash decision that kids often do and volunteered for the U.S. Air Force. I arrived in San Antonio Texas, a smart assed, Chicago bred, kid with long hair. Who would have thought that the boy from Vienna would end up trying to look like Elvis? I guess I was *All Shook Up*.

The first day of basic training we were all standing at attention and the Drill Instructor for some reason focused on me. He came over and stuck his face close to mine and I can still smell his breath, coffee and cigarettes mixed together with his cheap aftershave. It was probably "Hai Karate".

He yelled "Hey Jocko pull your stomach in. You look pregnant."

Not thinking, as I did a lot in those days, I mumbled under my breath, "Yeah I got screwed when I enlisted."

Well the crusty DI must have had dog ears because he heard me. I was *busted* and had hell to pay. I ended up on KP for 3 weeks and for the duration of basic training my new name was "Jocko".

Many years later I was running my own waste paper trading company and in another one of my weak moments, for some reason probably old fashioned greed motivated, I made a classic business error, I didn't follow my own rules and I got burned. During a tight market I shorted one of my regular customers and shipped some tonnage off for a higher price than I quoted them. Some questions were raised and to make a long story short, I was *busted*. I owned up to the customer and it took me almost a year to get his trust back. Clyde is a musician and he speaks of tempo, keeping your rhythm. Getting busted for saying or doing something "stupid" is one of the ways that you lose your tempo.

Tom has a set of bongos in his office and he actually plays them as he reflects on the 1950's and the Beat Generation, the time when I entered the service. One of our best customers is based near Lowell, Massachusetts, the hometown of Jack Kerouac. Tom loves to walk the streets there and visit some of Kerouac's old haunts when he is in the area.

His favorite quote of Kerouac's from <u>On The Road</u> written in 1957 is:

- The only people for me are the mad ones, the ones who are mad to live, mad to talk, mad to be saved, desirous of everything at the same time, the ones who never yawn or say a

commonplace thing, but burn, burn, burn like fabulous yellow roman candles exploding like spiders across the stars...

Clyde reminded us of what Mark Knopfler wrote in a song on the Dire Straits album, *On Every Street*, "If you want to run cool, you've got to run on heavy, heavy fuel."

That makes sense. Burn, but don't burn out. In the movie *War Games* the fictional military supercomputer W.O.P.R. (War Operation Plan Response) had to learn *how* to learn. Even when I was getting busted, I was learning. I still am. The message is clear. You will make mistakes in life, so fess up, take your lumps, don't bellyache too much, live with the consequences and be trained from each experience. Learn how to learn. I certainly did.

You caught me red handed.

Now do you want to join me?

Clyde says-"I'll join you for a drink!"

Hickey makes a toast-"I'll drink to that!"

Chapter 18
Free Tickets and Gateways to Adventure

I got a free ticket in the mail the other day. Being a frequent flyer has its rewards. I love the ambiance in an airport where we carry ourselves and a few necessities to faraway places for fun and profit. Tom and Clyde and I have collectively traveled tens of millions of miles. We often talk about how each trip is just like the first one.

Tom's love of travel and his love of Hemingway resulted in an article written about him by journalist, Candy Webb in his local newspaper back in 2007. I wanted to share it with you because it encompasses our sense of adventure in what we write and what we do.

Growing up in a small town in East Tennessee, he idolized American authors like Henry David Thoreau, Jack London and Ernest Hemingway. He read everything he could get his hands on that they had written and vowed one day to make his living the way they did, with words and ideas. And he does. Hendersonville author Tom Hicks recently completed his sixth published book.

This latest publication pays homage to one of Hicks' all time favorite authors, Hemingway. It is titled, "My Way or the Hemingway."

The plot involves the death of Hicks, who is granted one wish by Peter on his way to the pearly gates. Hicks wishes for a day with Hemingway, and the wish is granted.

"We travel around, we sit and talk, we discuss fishing, life, just about everything," said Hicks. "And then suddenly he is gone, and I am left reflecting on what we talked about and how his words apply to my life."

Hicks knew he wanted to become a writer at the tender age of 10.

"I lived in this small town, and the lady who ran the library introduced me to the wonderful world of literature," said Hicks. "There isn't much to do there except fish, so I did a lot of reading."

According to Hicks, he had a special place that he would go to sit on a large rock overlooking a sleepy creek and read his days away.

"I knew then that I would be a writer, but I took the advice of Hemingway, who once said; 'Before you write it, live it', so I hit the hold button on writing for years while I traveled and lived things to write about."

That decision paid off. Today, Hicks takes his experiences and turns them into stories for the public.

Whether it is co-authoring a life story with a Holocaust survivor, writing about his experiences growing up with philosophers who sat on porches and whittled while they expounded on life, or traveling the world with Hemingway, Hicks brings life to new ideas and metaphors.

"I think that is one of the beauties of living," said Hicks. "As we get older we begin to see the metaphoric examples of

everyday life and we learn to appreciate and enjoy those things."

Hicks believe literature is to be enjoyed by everyone and that there should not be an ability to censor what is read.

"Literature is so precious to me," said Hicks. "Whether it is good, bad or ugly, you have to read it, digest it and interpret it as it applies to your life and your experiences."

Hicks believes that the books people read during their lifetime, even as children, remain with them throughout their journey and when the time is right and the story from the past applies to a current situation, one can use it as a guide.

"I sit before you as a 53-year-old man today," he said. "But I am also still that ten-year-old boy of yesterday. All of our life experiences, including what we read, helps us become who we are in life."

Hicks enjoys learning about his favorite authors and their lives as well. In particular he is fascinated with Hemingway.

"We have completely different personalities," said Hicks. "But I enjoy learning about who he was and what brought him to be able to write the way he wrote. He didn't want to lead the reader down his path, he wanted the characters to have their own personalities and let the reader follow them instead. That is something I try to do as well."

Hicks recently participated in a Hemingway look-alike contest in Key West, Florida and enjoyed the experience.

"I could look around and see 200 Hemingways," said Hicks. "It was amazing."

While he has a personality that is completely different than Hemingway's reported gruff attitude, Hicks and Hemingway do have something in common.

They share a common bond of innate and impressive intelligence about human nature and life.

One walks away from a conversation with Hicks knowing one has been given several philosophical ideas to ponder long after the conversation has ended.

His warm, easygoing manner puts you right at ease, and his ability to verbalize ideas that bring the meaning of life into focus will astound even the most cynical audience.

"I enjoy life and figuring out the meaning of our existence," said Hicks. "All of it, the good, the bad, the hard and the easy are steps toward that understanding."

He is a family man, who refers to children as the gift that keeps on giving.

"It is really great when you have talked to your children about some of your beliefs or ideas, and then your wife tells you that she heard one of them repeating what you said to friends and telling them that their dad taught that to them. It feels great."

In order to turn out seven books while also putting on theater productions, acting in the local Steeple Players Theater group and spending time with family, Hicks adheres to a strict writing schedule.

"I get up early every morning and spend an hour thinking," said Hicks. "It allows ideas to come to me and be explored. Then I make sure I write 1,000 words every day. If I miss a day I double up the next day so I maintain that pace."

Hicks advises anyone with a desire to write to use self-discipline to get the words on the page.

"Even if you only write a page a day, "he said. "In a few months, you have written a book. The discipline is important if you want to get it done."

We should never ever underestimate one of the greatest freedoms we have and that is the ability to be mobile. I love to come and I love to go. Further, we should never underestimate the power of words to express who we are. The discipline it takes to journal your experiences is one I encourage you to develop.

In his book, *The Greatest Salesman in the World*, Og Mandino says, "If I must be a slave to habits, let me be a slave to good habits." Recording one's life experiences is a good habit. So, quite simply write it down, key it in, whatever. Like photographs, your journals are memories worth saving and that is greater than any other measure of wealth.

I am this 80 year old man who sits before you today. But, I am also that 7 year old boy who escaped Hitler and the Holocaust with his family on the last ship leaving Rotterdam after making my way from Austria some 70 plus years ago. All of my life experiences have made me who I am today.

To paraphrase a song that Clyde, a songwriter himself often sings, I say that winning or losing in real life or a game is an adventure in sunshine and rain. That's not bad. I guess I'm a bit of a poet or songwriter myself. I guess we all are.

So, I'll sum it up like this. When I can be free on a free ticket, it's like double dipping your way to adventure.

Remember what Casey Stengel said, "Old-timers, weekends, and airplane landings are alike. If you can walk away from them, they're successful." Eight decades and I am still on my feet. The *luck is still running good, Papa Hemingway*.

Chapter 19
Contraptions and Weekend Devices

"There aren't enough days in the weekend," thought Rod Schmidt and I couldn't agree more but a Saturday morning is just a tremendous way to start. I never fail to tell my friends and family and whoever is listening on Friday night that tomorrow is my day off. So here I sit either doing or thinking about what I am doing. Now that's something. I am working out the kinks from a week that included a long day when I was pushed to the limits of my civility.

Calvin & Hobbes honestly had it right when they conversed-

"- "I've been thinking Hobbes –"

- "…On a weekend?"

- "Well, it wasn't on purpose…"

Life may indeed be a cartoon especially on weekends, the time when a man can take his wife out for a hot dog and say "What the heck!"

One thing leads to another you may remember I wrote. As a boy I liked literary heroes like Robin Hood and the way we know him owes a great deal to Ivanhoe. Robin Hood from Locksley becomes Robin of Locksley, alias Hood. The Saxon-Norman conflict is made a major theme by Sir Walter Scott. Actually Sir Walter avoids the practice of depicting Robin as an evicted nobleman. Robin's exploit of splitting a rival arrow in an archery contest appears for the first time in Ivanhoe. Now I have my heroes, everyone should, but heroes like Robin Hood are flawed in many ways just like you and me.

So there we have our hero in tights, nevertheless the stuff for movieland and in the end, Ivanhoe and Rowena marry and live a long and happy life together and probably went out for hot dogs on weekends.

As the Bard would say, All's well that ends well or as Hickey's Grandma would say, "It is what it is and it ain't what it ain't," or was that Clyde's favorite folk singer, John Prine? Or maybe it was Tom Dundee.

I have owned and operated a lot of contraptions. Contraptions do some remarkable things and even surprise their inventors. Orville Wright once said, "No flying machine will ever fly from New York to Paris." So machines can exceed our greatest expectations. I rely on devices to make up for my flaws. I have spent a career with all sorts of devices to recycle paper and therefore make me some dough. I buy the latest gadgets because I like the latest and the greatest. Back in the 1990's, The Sharper Image catalog was the impetus for a teleconference about what we were going to order that month, right before sales projections and cash flow analysis. You can't let business get in the way of pleasure all the time, can you?

I sit among my machines that do stuff or make stuff and I ride in them or on them and I am in awe of how they are reflections of raw materials made by God and built to serve us after a man or woman observed the world around them and said I have an idea.

As you may remember I love any thought that becomes a thing; a damn useful thing-A very good thing. Contraptions fuel my dreams and take me there like Captain Kirk on Star Trek.

Million of miles ago and many years ago, I saw it on a wall somewhere; that Pan AM poster from the 30's that shows a Boeing 314 Clipper coming in for a landing in Tahiti. It stirred up my juices and today I get excited every time I get on a plane going somewhere....anywhere...which happens a lot.

Thoreau would say, "We need only travel enough to give our intellects an airing."

My brain cells have been aired out for the last seventy plus years and I find that the desire to hop on that metaphorical Clipper is still as intense as it ever was.

To change Baldwin's quote a little, "I met a lot of people in my travels. I even encountered myself." Clyde would say, "I had a dream I was awake and when I woke up I was asleep."

These days I like to pack as little as possible and I keep a toiletry bag ready to rock and I can be ready to roll in minutes.

"He who would travel happily must travel light." When Tom read me this quote, I agreed with Antoine. Sometimes the challenge is to leave *stuff* behind and as Solzhenitsyn would say "Let your memory be your travel bag." Or as George Carlin said, "...All you need in life is a little place for your *stuff*. Your house is just a place to keep your *stuff*. If you didn't have so much *stuff*, you wouldn't need a house." That's enough on *stuff*.

I always wanted to travel as a kid and I have. Helen Keller's advice has stuck with me on my gathering of frequent flyer, rental car and hotel awards. "Life is either a daring adventure or nothing."

Okay, one more point on *stuff*. You see the less *stuff* you carry is like shedding pounds on a diet, you just feel lighter (hint: because you are) and less encumbered which prompted Dedman to write, "They don't put luggage racks on a hearse." You see, those contraptions and devices must be fun and as I said earlier useful, though that may be saying one and the same.

Travel is a metaphor for your journey called LIFE. As the old bible hero, Job said, and I paraphrase according to Tom, "I came here naked as a baby and that's the way I will leave." Clyde sings a song about that when we're together.

Now that's traveling light. Do it with style and enjoy your contraptions like the latest tablet computer or smart phone or better yet, the latest driver designed to improve your golf game. Most importantly have peace on your journey and blessings on each and every real or metaphorical weekend.

"The best tool to improve your score
is a pencil with an eraser."

Chapter 20
Reminiscing and Sharing

"Never be afraid to sit awhile and think." Lorraine Hansberry wrote in *A Raisin in the Sun*. The window has been a metaphor for me my whole life. As a boy I looked out the window of my Vienna Apartment and wondered what might happen to me. As a man, it was the same with business as I sat in hotel rooms and watched the city and towns below.

Clyde is one of the best interviewers I know and I love it when he uses his journalism name- RW Pickel. He is like one of those intrepid reporters of yesteryear and he is so insightful. He thinks about everything he does with great intent. The other day, I found an article he wrote for us and it summed up our second run of the stage production performed in 2008 beautifully.

When Hendersonville businessman Tom Hicks first began to notice how his partner enjoyed looking out the windows of hotels on their many business trips together, he was curious about this obsession. One day, his partner Peter "Otto" Abeles would tell him his story. And that he did. The result was Otto, the Boy at the Window, a book they co-authored and published in 2001. Since then, this story has taken on a life of its own.

In 2005, while performing in the stage play Scrooge, Tom met Mt. Juliet playwright Bill Dorian, who was the narrator in the production. For some time Hicks and Abeles had been discussing the possibility of having Pete's story developed into a stage play. This chance meeting of Hicks and Dorian resulted in the stage version of Abeles' story. It debuted in Nashville in

2007 with excellent reviews and was named "Best Original Holocaust Drama" by Martin Brady of the Nashville Scene. This May and June, Otto Productions will once again bring this story to life with shows in Mt. Juliet and Hendersonville.

Abeles was born in the early 30's in Vienna, Austria and was raised by an emotionally abusive mother and a father who took no real interest in him or his older brother, Heinz Robert. The family lived in an upper middle class Jewish neighborhood with all the modern comforts, including a chauffeur and a maid. The year prior to the Anschluss his father had even been named the "Businessman of the Year" for the city of Vienna. But, on March 12, 1938, the Abeles' world and that of all Jewish families in Austria was about to suddenly change for the worse. After nearly losing everything, including their lives, Peter's father was able to make contact with two American Abeles' families who would ultimately sponsor them and bring them to Chicago.

To have a friend who thinks like you do is a great blessing.

Adam Smith is on my best thinkers list along with John Locke and the Greeks and Tommy Jefferson. In his classic The Wealth of Nations, Smith stated what I think needs to be restated:

"It is not from the benevolence of the butcher, the brewer, or the baker that we expect our dinner, but from their regard to their own interest. We address ourselves, not to their humanity but to their self-love, and never talk to them of our own necessities but of their advantages." Further to that, Smith wrote that the "real price of everything … is the toil and trouble of acquiring it" as influenced by its scarcity. Like we often say, noting worthwhile comes easy. I add that desire is a motivator of many things, even romance. Many today have lost the passion to go after the dream and would rather sit back and let others make them comfortable in their mediocrity. Classical economics focused on the tendency of markets to move to long-run equilibrium. Smith was wary of monopolies and government but ultimately knew that the markets operate by natural law.

You are a corporation of ONE. Run your company like a good CEO. It is not greedy to have self-love. It is natural. And when you love yourself first, take stock in it (preferred shares of course), then full of that love, you are able to give the overflow to others. The same applies to wealth. Once you have some, then you can share it by buying the goods and services that others have to sell.

I want everyone to have it all including me and of course, you. WE DESERVE IT!

"If you insist on putting me on hold,
you can at least play a little Strauss."

Chapter 21
Reflecting is the Business of Man -
Thinks Shakespeare and Otto

I was thinking about a monthly meeting of *The Forum Club* of South West Florida that I had recently attended. The Forum Club is nationally recognized for its outstanding speaker program. The featured speaker that particular day was Ronald A. DePhino, MD, who is a leading scientist in the fields of cancer and aging. His research has focused on the close link between cancer and aging as well as the genetic basis of cancer and how such knowledge can enable the accurate development of effective targeted cancer therapies and optimize the treatment of patients with cancer. Dr. DePhino's recent discovery that the aging process can be reversed captured worldwide media attention and was cited among the top 10 scientific discoveries of 2010 by TIME Magazine.

His speech brought back fond memories of my deceased brother Dr. Robert H. Abeles who was a well known research scientist and teacher. I sent Dr. DePhino an e-mail asking if he knew my brother. His answer was *I did not know your brother personally but, of course; I am familiar with his seminal contributions to biochemistry. His stature was iconic.*

Robert was my hero, my friend and supporter but most of all, he was my brother. It was with his help that I was able to deal with my abusive mother and uninterested father. I remember when, I was 8 and he was 13, lying in bed crying after being severely scolded and sent to bed early without dessert for a minor infraction of "bad" manners.

Robert snuck a piece of chocolate cake and brought it to my bedroom. My mother would have literally come unglued had she caught him. He wiped away my tears and before long we were talking and laughing together. He was good at that. I'll never forget what he told me. He said "Otto if we stick together there is nothing in life we can't accomplish". Years later when I had my stuttering problem in High School, he was there to help me. Just like in Vienna, Austria he was there for me. Robert was always there for me.

I have been thinking a lot about that meeting held with Tom, Clyde and William Dorian. Bill has been writing stage plays, including "Otto", and acting and directing for live theater for 35 years. *True Brothers* was the name we all agreed on and it was aptly entitled because it captured the long term relationship I had with my brother. It was the further development of the storyline about me, Otto and my brother Heinz Robert. At the meeting, I told everyone how pleased I was that my brother's story would also be told because quite frankly without Robert, I would never have been able to make it through those early years.

Those moments we experience in life, the good and the bad, make us who we are. So, use the richness of your past to fill your soul with loving memories and use those moments to help you realize your dreams. They will help guide you to your next destination on your incredible journey.

I was thinking the other afternoon how much I do love to take the train. But the romance in travel is perhaps dying because the destination has become more important than the journey. Clyde likens it to acting. When he goes to audition, he certainly wants to get the job. But, he focuses on the audition as an end in itself and if he ultimately gets the job, that just becomes another leg of the journey *and* he gets a paycheck. But, the important thing is to enjoy the process, the *journey*.

At any speed, the purpose of a trip, long or short is to provide another entry into one's *Travel Journal*, a vivid memory of time well spent on yet another adventure of some sort. When my brother and I with our parents were making our escape from Austria on that train filled with Gestapo Agents, as we traveled to Holland to make the last boat out of Rotterdam, there was a bond based on fear but also entrenched in the hope of a better day that we both eventually realized.

If the technology of modern life is a partner in that endeavor, then that is better for my brother and I too believe in the advancement of society on all levels. On the other hand, as Confucius would say it does not matter how slowly you go, so long as you do not stop. So, I do not intend to stop and I will certainly never stop loving Robert. Not a day goes by that I don't think of my brother. I really miss Heinz Robert. It's okay to never stop missing the ones you love.

"Hey Will, Have I got a line for you?
To be Otto or not to be Otto that is the question.
Feel free to use that...for a small fee!"

Chapter 22
The Case for Paper and Hard Work

This week, a friend reminded me of *"noblesse oblige"* that if you claim to be noble you must then behave nobly. As Tom says, "...learning much when I am riding high and learning more when the well is dry." Being noble is not subject to circumstances. A noble one should act in a fashion that is the same as the position that one has earned and as Aristotle advised, "Practice is the best of all instructions."

We should expect it from our leaders but more importantly, ourselves.

Van Gogh wrote, "Poetry surrounds us everywhere, but putting it on paper is, alas, not *as* easy as looking at it."

Paper has never been a substitute for the real thing but it is a way of recording it and allowing it to be shared with the world. So are high tech advancements.

Recently we are seeing the demise of the printed catalog, the daily newspaper, books, and direct mail, as well as many forms of traditional advertising which coupled with the economic downturn has made it a rough go for printers, the descendents of Ben Franklin's tradition of the printed word.

Likewise, the market for recyclables has been hurt as well. So I do have an agenda. But consider the never ending market for tissue and toilet paper and paper towels which is where your recyclables normally end up.

I would like to make the case for a hybrid society that uses technology but also understands the uniqueness of a hard document. It is secure. It is far more transportable and durable in many ways such as the book on the back of your toilet, the soft cover you carry to the beach, the newspaper that you are not afraid to drip a little coffee on, and the magazine or catalog you can't wait to run to the mailbox and retrieve. There is something childlike and beautiful about that I think.

We visit hundreds of small and mid-sized printers every year. Many are family businesses and employees work at these companies for their entire career. Please keep buying newspapers. Keep those catalogs and magazines coming and cherish the art of advertising which says so much about our culture.

Tom was telling me that he has an abundance of old luggage stickers and old magazine covers around his office because what he feels he is today is a direct result of what others have done.

I love my computer and my mobile phone and I use a navigation system, but I carry an Atlas and I work the NY Times crossword with glee and I believe that there is room enough for the past and the future in my present. Long live Paper!

Sisyphus was condemned to an eternity of hard work. And it was frustrating labor at that. His task was to roll a big rock to the top of a hill. Only every time Sisyphus got to the summit, the darn boulder rolled back down again.

What lesson do we learn from this old myth? Is the work alone enough? Camus would remark, "The struggle itself towards the heights is enough to fill a man's heart. One must imagine Sisyphus happy."

There could be opportunity at every step of the way but it doesn't rear its head as opportunity. It looks like something else.

For as the great Edison would conclude, "Opportunity is missed by most because it is dressed in overalls and looks like work."

When you're in the recycling biz and the presses roll,
so do you.

Hickey and Clyde say "Silver dollars are round.
So let 'em roll!"

Chapter 23
Our Towns

Have you ever been told you think quickly on your feet? It can be a good trait or a little on the downside. Here's my theory. As I go through life in a cowboy hat or a Brooks Brothers suit, traveling at the speed of thought as it races me and those around me through worlds of illusion, it seems we are all searching for "the" answer to whatever problems come our way. One solution that will be the cure for everything and then when it doesn't happen, we can get a little frustrated.

Now the further I move away from reaching the understanding that the one true source of freedom already lives within me, right where I am regardless of age or position. In short, I had it then. I have it now. Dorothy learned a big lesson in Oz when she concluded "If I ever go looking for my heart's desire again; I won't look any further than my own back yard. Because if it isn't there; I never really lost it to begin with!"

I go visit Tom a lot in the *little* town where he lives on the northeast side of Nashville. Actually, it's not really a *little* town, but it is a suburb of a city so for my purposes we'll call it *little*. I feel almost as at home there as Tom does. As I have mentioned earlier, Tom and Clyde are actors and as he reminisced about a play from high school, Tom related the following story to me about the importance of a sense of community.

"I travel extensively and on most of my trips, business or pleasure, I am surprised at how often I proudly mention the

*community where I live to others. I am also amazed at how nostalgic I have become. The other day, for example, I thought back fondly to 1971 when I attended high school and remembered reading the role of the Stage Manager who serves as the narrator in Thornton Wilder's **Our Town**, the classic stage production that is a beautiful piece of work depicting an average American community just like ours in many ways.*

*If you can recall, the story takes place in a small town in New Hampshire one hundred years ago but its timeless theme speaks volumes to us today. It caused me to embrace and discuss the traditions that make our own town, Hendersonville, a truly American community in its own rite. We have a remarkable place here. For instance, I recently appeared in **Footloose** with a great cast of local actors, dancers, and musicians at Steeple Players Theatre. In case you hadn't noticed, your friends and neighbors are quite talented. Anyhow, the three acts of Mr. Wilder's play analyze the reality of ordinary folks like you and me, specifically explored as they go about the three acts of Daily Life, Love and Marriage, and Death and Eternity.*

*We should each come to realize that seemingly commonplace activities are actually very important. Going to school or work, mowing the yard or planting flowers, spending a day on the lake or shopping, and reading the local newspaper define what it means to live and the people around you help you appreciate this wonderful life in many ways. We are all connected. The first act of the play, **Our Town**, culminates as George and his sister, Rebecca, look out their window and up at the sky and wonder about the meaning of the universe. My wife and I have reclined in our little boat on many summer nights and done exactly the same thing right here, anchored on Old Hickory Lake.*

When the play's star-crossed lovers, George and Emily marry and he gives up his dream of going away to seek his fortune, it is revealed that when you meet someone special it is worth the sacrifice to stay home with that person who 'likes you enough to be interested in your character' and while no community is perfect, when the bells toll like they do at the local church they toll for one and all whether you are in Grover's Corners or in the town where you live. Love and Marriage is why we do what we do. It brings out the very best in people like the ensuing miracle of babies being born. Here like there, they are taken care of by a good doctor prompting Emily to say "I'd rather have my children healthy than bright."

Most of us today would say we want both and thanks to good schools and hospitals it is possible here. After a trip, my kids still say 'it is good to be home.' I could not agree more. That brings me to the uncomfortable subject of death, an everyday occurrence for us humans here and now and in Mr. Wilder's mythical town as well. I rarely go through our town that I do not see images of people leaving us as I go to funerals and pass by cemeteries. As I age it becomes more apparent and in some ways, more real.

After dying an untimely death, in spirit form, Emily tells us in the play that life for husband George will never be the same without her, adding, 'Live people don't understand, do they?' She's right as we often don't realize how wonderful life here really is."

My prayer for us, my fellow citizens is to wake up and smell the coffee, or the toast, or the roses, or whatever it is that arouses your senses to a newfound love for life and to a newfound appreciation for your town. Clyde grew up in a town of two thousand people. There are twenty to thirty times more people than that in any given football stadium on any given Sunday in any given city in this country. I live in Naples, Florida and Bethesda, Maryland and I love them both. Each is small and each is big and in a special way, both are unique.

In my play, Otto discovered the value of living life in the present moment when he came to Chicago after leaving Europe. Likewise in Wilder's play, Emily discovered that life is to be treasured in the little town where she lived and all of you should do so in the town where you live. I will put it simply in her words, "Every, every minute." Yes, life is made up of minutes and each one is as special as the one before it. It has been said *Chicago ain't no sissy town* and I learned a sissy wouldn't last long there or in the end, anywhere. America's towns are full of gutsy people living life on their own terms giving their towns an exceptional flavor. When I visit a town and discover a new restaurant, I am not only nourishing my body and enjoying the local fare but I am in a sense tasting the town itself. Tom and I always end up finding a place with a view and end up talking about this and that and soaking up the last few moments of the day before we go off to bed and rekindle our dreams. Those dreams contain all the places we have ever been and maybe all of the places we will one day go. Dreams lost are never found so never stop dreaming.

Walt Whitman was right.
"A great city is that which has the greatest men and women."

Hickey to Otto on leaving Otto's Old Chicago Haunt-
The Golden Ox

"And even now she beats her head against the bars in the same old way and wonders if there is a bigger place the railroads run to from Chicago where maybe there is romance and big things and real dreams that never go smash."

— *Carl Sandburg*

Chapter 24
A little communication with no strings attached

Most everything I know of has a price tag attached to it. Clyde once remarked, "The cool thing about prayer is there is no charge for the minutes." Yep, no strings attached and that is not true for everything in this technological age.

Tom laughs about the fact that nearly fifty years ago, his friend Tony and he used two cans and about twenty feet of string to attempt to communicate with makeshift phones, our latest technology at the time. After numerous attempts, they laid the cans down, talked to each other with slightly elevated voices and determined that they would walk to Disney's store and get a grape soda pop. Made me think if someone is nearby perhaps the simplest way to communicate is the best. So I am sending out a universal plea. I will call it Otto's advice. Every now and then would you please just talk to me? Don't text. Don't email. Call if you must but better yet, leave the mobile phone in the car and sit down, look me in the eye and talk.

I love technology and use all forms in my business and personally I blog and use social networking most every day. It's all good. But it is no substitute for looking a man in the eye and it is no replacement for a firm handshake or better yet the classic hug. As I told you, I haven't always been good at hugging but I have learned it really works.

In the final analysis, I like people more than tools. Tools are a means to an end. And the end is to connect with all of your brothers and sisters beginning here in your own community.

"Reach out and touch somebody's hand" Diana Ross sang and she was right on. I can't tell you how many times I have answered the person next to me at an airport when they were actually talking to someone on a Bluetooth while staring into space. I have stopped being embarrassed and keep saying "I am fine" until they acknowledge me whether they want to or not.

After thousands of years it is still about human touch. Researchers in Utah found that a warm touch — the non-sexual supportive kind which may surprise screenwriters and novelists — tempers stress and blood pressure, adding to a growing body of research on how emotions affect health. The study found that supportive and caring touch lowers stress hormones and blood pressure, particularly among men and we men all know that we need it the most. After all, we have been fighting among ourselves and starting wars while the womenfolk cleaned up our messes.

Conversation is a dying art form. I mean real conversation, the kind where you say what you think, not what you think others want you to say and how about having the courage to speak your mind as well as listening openly to the views and ideas of others? And by all means the art of conversation includes the ability to pay attention to others as well as the ability to speak. Clyde teaches acting and is constantly emphasizing to his students the philosophy of Sanford Meisner, who said, "The foundation of acting is the reality of doing. The 'realty of doing' means when you do something, you really do it rather than pretend that you're doing it." Clyde highlights that the best acting comes from the truth. In other words, an actor's job is to tell the *truth*. And, one does this by practicing what one does in real life and that is to "listen, feel, and react." That's how we connect. It takes practice and it takes time. I know. No one has any time for such nonsense. Well, amazingly, "Time stays long enough for those who use it", advised Leonardo Da Vinci. I believe in magic. So how about you and I magically finding a way to create some time? Is that any more remarkable than sending typed words through thin air?

And at the risk of being contradictory sometimes you say the most when you say nothing. Sometimes you just need to be there with someone. Gandhi thought that "Happiness is when what you think, what you say, and what you do are in harmony." When you are sitting there peacefully with a friend, thinking about peaceful things and perhaps watching a hummingbird do its thing that alone says multitudes about who you are. And the very fact that you took the time and that you aren't harping about what you bought or where you've been or how much you know. Guess what? It's okay to just be with someone.

I love the words of the song, *When You Say Nothing at All*, written by Don Schlitz and Paul Overstreet. Keith Whitley's recording of it took it to the top of the Billboard Hot Country Singles in 1988 and Alison Krauss' version was a top 10 country hit in 1995. It has always been and always will be good advice to sometimes say nothing and that often says more than a thousand words.

Tom was telling me a story about his early life. He said, "I did not have the greatest relationship with my Dad when I was a teenager. He was a smoking, drinking, gambler and could be gruff. I wasn't quite sure if he loved me or not. But when it snowed, he would light up like a kid and make me hop in his old truck and we would ride up to the top of Vowel Mountain, just him and me, and we would watch the snow fall in the woods near where he grew up. We didn't say much but those few times formed my lasting impression of him and laid the groundwork for forgiveness for all the other slights I felt. No device could replace those trips up that old mountain. You just had to be there. It's true 'the smallest distance is too great, and the greatest distance can be bridged.' It just takes a little more effort than hitting a few keystrokes."

The handwritten note or a well penned letter is yet another art form that is a more refined way to express complicated or heartfelt thoughts. I often hear of something negative or personal expressed in a text or an email and someone was hurt or offended when at the very least a phone call would have been far more appropriate and in most cases, a face to face conversation where respect and genuine honesty would have been the best choice.

Perhaps a mistake was made for expediency's sake. Or perhaps the meaning is completely misunderstood. Shamefully, here we are several thousand years down the line and we still have trouble doing the most natural thing of all, talking things out. Well all I repeatedly ask is every once in a while, stop by and speak to me like a fellow citizen on a similar path with common goals. I would really appreciate that and I will try to return the favor, if not in person in my prayers and there will absolutely be no charge.

There is some truth perhaps in that old saying the best things in life are free. Some things don't cost anything or very little in dollars. But the investment in time and energy often called sweat equity may be even more expensive. Freedom is like that. What you want most for yourself you have to work equally hard to get for others. Step out of the thundering herd and be strong.

Be who you always expected yourself to be with no strings attached. Join together with your friends and unite in doing what needs to be done always realizing it is never enough and keep in mind that every now and then you have to tell the naysayers to either be productive or be quiet.

Gentlemen: I propose we live like Gerry Spence suggests for freedom seekers: *When we acknowledge the kingdom of the self, we will no longer accept slavery either for ourselves or for others. All in favor say "Aye" All opposed "Shut up"*

Signed, sealed, and delivered by Otto

Hickey puts in his two cents worth with the wisdom of Spinoza,

"...all things excellent are as difficult as they are rare."

Chapter 25
The Bonus

Everyone likes to get a bonus, a little extra something to sweeten the pot. But you never know what that bonus is or what form it might take. For instance, I had gotten off the plane the other day and Tom was there to greet me. The obvious question is "How was your flight?" The obvious answer is "Fine." We sat at Tootsie's Orchid Lounge in the airport and chatted for a few minutes while we planned our day.

Tom laughed and said, "You know, Pete, in 1987, I believe it was, I was one or two planes ahead of the Northwest flight that departed from Detroit and crashed and all we saw was a fireball as we banked and turned so we could see the rental car area where it ended up I believe. I think a lone little girl survived in what has been described as a miracle. As a million mile flyer on several airlines, I went through one period of a few months where I was hypersensitive to sounds but otherwise, I trust the skill of the pilots and while I am a man of science feel I am wrapped up in a destiny kismet fate sort of adventurous Indiana Jones type of existence. Every day is a bonus, a Divine perk of which I am extremely grateful. I have little patience for people who say they are bored. Are they kidding me?"

He was right. Boredom is a sign of laziness. Let me explain. As I have tried to stress, ideas and opportunities morph into real "things". The biggest problem seems to lie in the fact that most of us are inconsistent in our follow through and even worse our determination of what to do with our time allotment, the biggest bonus of all.

Now thinking is not a part time job but a full time sense of self. We all forget details but if the big picture concepts wane then they were never about being fulfilled. They were just talk. Talk is cheap. Yeah there are plenty of good things in store but not if you don't even care enough to handle them with care.

Tom is a lover of lighthouses and he loves to talk about climbing the many steps at the Cape Hatteras Lighthouse. He declares that it is a walk worth taking and gives one a new found appreciation of the important job the keeper of the flame had. The concept of safe passage is a paradox for there is no such thing as safety for we earthlings are pilgrims on a sphere with a molten center and a surface of mostly water with volatile atmospheric conditions as we go zooming through space at mind-bending speeds all the while under siege by microscopic dangers. Cheating death on a daily basis is our fate and finding peace in this chaos is indeed informative and fulfilling.

Anyone who knows me knows I'm a realist. We all need money. Back in my early days, I discovered in business that you can run out of anything but cash. Money is, after all a tool, and if one keeps that perspective in mind, well, then the acquisition of it and the loss of it becomes a game. A serious game sometimes, but a game just the same, and in a capitalist system like ours; it can be an enormous amount of fun. As the famous Vaudevillian comic, Ralph Hitchcock once mused, "A man isn't poor if he can still laugh." I like to laugh all the way to the bank.

I am a man who loves mystery and miracles and accept each. But practically speaking in most cases, what we call a mystery is a fully functioning law that is not understood, perhaps misunderstood. Sometimes what we label a miracle is a law that is operating in a perfectly normal way. Figuring stuff out is a skill that will get you those bonuses I've been talking about. It got my father a passage out of a dangerous country and a fresh start here in the USA.

His rugged individualism embodies the phrase- *Tu ne cede mali sed contra audentior ito* which is Latin for "Do not give in to evil but proceed ever more boldly against it." I like that! It's kind of like the best defense is a good offense. It's about staying on the attack.

These thoughts attributed to Virgil are also the expressed motto of the Ludwig Von Mises Institute and the thought process of the Austrian School which emerged in the city where I was born and embrace the concept of individualism have both intrigued me & continues to challenge me.

As Von Mises would say "What transformed the stagnant conditions of the good old days into the activism of capitalism were not changes in the natural sciences and in technology, but the adoption of the free enterprise principle."

While admonishing his new class, Professor John Keating in the film *Dead Poets Society* is remembering those who have gone before and encouraging his new class about the great potential within them. As they are closely considering the old photographs he says, "....if you listen real close, you can hear them whisper their legacy to you. Go on, lean in. Listen, you hear it? - - Carpe - - hear it? - - Carpe, carpe diem, seize the day boys, make your lives extraordinary." Each day is indeed a miracle so carpe diem, seize the day and if you are both lucky and good you might just get a bonus; another day in this beautiful world with a few bucks in your pocket to spend.

Seize the day, people, and cheat death any chance you get.
Death is an asshole.

-Otto Diem-

Chapter 26
Props and Scenery

As a Writer and Producer and even as a businessman, I love props. I have been thinking of special props that all of us guys should use to make life more darn interesting:

An Eye Patch-like the Hathaway Man from the old ads I used to love in Gentlemen's Quarterly and Esquire. He always sported a perfectly designed shirt. But I guess what I am saying is fit in but be unique.

For instance, Clyde recently sported a new Fedora at the Nashville Independent Film Festival as he covered a Red Carpet affair for a film starring Kris Kristofferson, where Kristofferson was joined by Emmylou Harris, Randy Scruggs, and a host of other country stars. He was told by a good pal that he certainly "looked" the part. He is an actor, after all.

Then there's the Meerschaum Pipe- a smoking instrument made of that beautiful white mineral from the Black Sea that Turks carve into exotic shapes that distinguish one from the ordinary.

And don't forget the Beret- red or black felt headgear reminding one of France or the Basque country with that moldable crown that can be worn in a variety of ways.

Tom loves the Bow Tie- Bow ties are in our popular culture items of refinement and sophistication but also a little mysterious as in James Bond. Absolutely no clip on is to be considered but wild patterns and tousled hair lend to the professorial air of extreme intelligence. Some famous bow tie wearers include Winston Churchill, Theodore Roosevelt, Groucho Marx, the former U.S. Surgeon General, C. Everett Koop. Then there's the unusual necktie worn by American Chemical Society Division of Medicinal Chemistry Hall of Fame member and multi award winner in his field, my brother Robert H. Abeles, Ph.D. His tie had chemical spots and never matched his outfit. Sometimes being eclectic is fashionable.

The Trench coat in Classic Khaki extremely wrinkled- Bogart style with belt loosely knotted and pockets filled with Jack Kerouac and Hemingway paperbacks is a classic look.

I am a Vodka man and Tom Likes Scotch Whiskey and then there's Clyde who prefers good Bourbon. We all like them poured neat in a very old glass and always sipped never gulped- It needs to be expertly quaffed and observed and swirled around for minutes if not hours as one contemplates the problems that life offers to be solved.

And a pair of classic reading glasses- Those little kind that hang on the end of the nose as you read an important document and are removed at random with the end strategically placed in the mouth during musing. Clyde likes this look because he is often told it makes him look intelligent. Looks can be deceiving.

And there are so many more like a walking cane, a colorful ascot, a worn messenger bag, anything from the J Peterman catalog, and a splash of authentic Bay Rum from the West Indies.

Yes the props of our life assist us in fulfilling the role that we "choose" to play. And, in reality it is a role we are not just playing, but actually living. Clyde likes to quote the great acting coach Constantin Stanislavski. In his book, *Building a Character*, Tortsov, the director, is addressing the class on physical characterization. He states, "The external characterization explains and illustrates and thereby conveys to your spectators the inner pattern of your part." In another of his books, *An Actor Prepares*, Tortsov talks of the actor being completely carried away with the play and says, "...regardless of his own will he lives the part, not noticing *how* he feels, not thinking about *what* he does, and it all moves of its own accord, subconsciously and intuitively." Interesting, don't you think? I like playing my part.

And then there is the backdrop for personal and professional adventures, the scenery. Tom and I found ourselves talking about rooftops, a classic setting. We recalled how we stood on the rooftop of a manufacturing facility and watched the planes fly in and out of Chicago. The November breeze was cold and biting. It penetrated every pore of our bodies.

We both stood near the rooftop of the Empire State Building early in Tom's career when we visited clients at a trade show and looked out at NYC when it was wholly intact and a warm spring breeze was blowing through the concrete jungle. It was amazing!

Tom recalled how he stood near the natural rooftop of the Cascades at Mount Hood, and before skiing down viewed the panoramic view of the Northwest U.S. in all of its winter glory, a mixture of whites and blues. That led him to a deck by the roof of his Key West rented condo and how he looked out as the Southern summer breeze heated his burned skin and soul which brought him to the rooftop of his rental car after visiting me in

Coronado. He was excited as he described the Pacific sun dropping into the sea near La Jolla after a day of clumsily riding waves on a Longboard with his bad knee and all.

Yes, those rooftop memories, one and all take me as well to times and places where my horizons were broadened and heightened. You see whether Europe of America or anywhere else I've been, there are rooftops to go to and see things you don't see at ground level because of the distractions that hinder your view.

I remember standing on the roof of a packaging plant with Tom and the crew superintendent on a frigid day in Green Bay, Wisconsin. The temperature was 30 below zero and it was windy and scary cold. I have never felt more alive. I was there in that moment doing business as usual. You never know where you might find yourself at any snapshot in time.

It has been written *wherever you go there you are.* So here we are. And just where is that?

Now that is an interesting question and so is "what I am going to do now?"

Clyde often says that the here and now is not there and then; but there and then was once here and now. Somehow that makes sense to me.

So, pick out your props, decide on your role, and choose your destination because Otto thinks you should go there wherever that is. And, when you are there just know that whether you are here or there you still are <u>you</u> at the wheel trudging on down the road to freedom and if you've figured that out; you're better off than most and if you haven't, well, you are in good company because it can take a very long time. I can personally attest to that.

You always have to be ready to constantly scrutinize the past and be as free-flowing as one of Heinz Robert's lab experiments where every failure brings you closer to a breakthrough. In fact what else do you have to do with your precious time anyway except live your life the best you can surrounded by those you love?

Eureka, my brother. We stuck together. We made it. By the way, where's that ugly tie with the chemical stain? My scientific guess is that it's probably in the laundry hamper with Einstein's socks.

Chapter 27
Behind the Scenes and
Growing Some Serious Gratitude

" Let us be grateful to people who make us happy; they are the charming gardeners who make our souls blossom," thought Marcel Proust. This is so true. Clyde reminded me that in his letter to the Hebrews, Paul the apostle writes in Chapter 13, verse 2, "Be not forgetful to entertain strangers: for thereby some have entertained angels unawares." That's something to think about.

You never know who you might meet and you certainly can never predict who might do something really amazing for you. We are usually more worried about who is going to screw us. But there are some really special people out there, millions of them and it might take time and a lot of hard work but eventually I think you meet them. Then you are really blown away and your life changes. I will try to explain. One day Bonnie and I were visiting Mike Ditka's restaurant in Naples. Bonnie nudged me toward him and I was speechless. Then a big hand was extended toward me and I shook it. I mumbled something. Bonnie took over and said that I really "loved" him. He smiled back and said he loved everybody. The following week I read he had thrown his cigar at the Pit Boss in Vegas. Sometimes love is expressed in remarkable ways.

Anyone who has been around a theatrical production knows that it is a very exciting time. Tom and I had a dream of producing this play and it was about to become a reality. The actual production of *Otto... the Play* adapted by William Dorian from our book had begun and in a short time casting was finished, rehearsals were scheduled, and all the other things necessary to stage a play were in motion. I reiterate these events because it was all so new to me and I couldn't wait for each new phase to start.

We were sitting in a small Mexican Restaurant in historic East Nashville, an artsy section of town where we were holding our rehearsals. We were having a bite to eat waiting to meet Thomas Kohann, the young man who was to be me, the young Otto in the play and his mother, Liliana. I looked up and there was a little boy standing there and he spoke to me with the refined European manners my mother expected from me. "Hi, I am Thomas and I am pleased to meet you." We chatted for a few minutes and then Tom introduced me to Liliana. I liked them both immediately.

A few days later I was at the first rehearsal which was about to start. According to the "experts" it went great. I could not imagine that a finished play could emerge from what seemed to me mass confusion but everyone seemed calm. Clyde has been in probably 50 or more plays since moving to Nashville and knows that it can often seem like things are a disaster, but after several weeks of piecing it together, magic usually happens on opening night. I was not so confident.

After a few more rehearsals I noticed Bill Dorian, who was also the director, was not pleased with the way the role of Ernst, my father was being portrayed; so I decided to put my two cents in and had a long talk with Shane Bridges, a remarkably talented actor playing Ernst. Being the gifted actor he is, Shane was trying to find the *humanity* in Ernst. The problem was, there really wasn't much humanity to find, at least not from my perspective until I discovered later a truth about my father that has changed me from the inside out. Sometimes it takes a lifetime to find even tidbits of the truth.

And since this story was being told as I recalled it, it was important to be truthful. As much as I respected my father, he was not really a very kind or loving man through the eyes of the boy reliving it and that is how I felt this man should be portrayed. After I expressed to Shane who this man was to me I think it really helped in his character development. As much as he wanted to show some kindness in his character portrayal of Ernst, he now began to understand there wasn't really any kindness to show and would find other ways to show the humanity in this man. And, that he did. Ultimately, Mr. Bridges gave a stellar performance and I was honored to have contributed to his performance. I shall never forget him.

Some days later, Tom and I visited Gene Hall, an old friend and business associate, who owned an equipment manufacturing and repair company. He had volunteered to help with the set design and construction. It turned out he was an angel in disguise. Remember Clyde's quote from Paul the Apostle? Without Gene we would have had to spend thousands of additional dollars, money we had not budgeted. Perhaps he was not really an angel, but to me he was.

Soon it was like a whirl wind of wardrobes, wall colors, window treatments, screens and one day the sound and lighting system appeared like magic. We used photos, video clips, and sound bites of the time period that played during set changes. This whole process was incredible and the apartment had so many images that made me cry when I saw it in its entirety the first time. It was like being in a time machine and walking into my apartment in Vienna with my brother and Adolph, our chauffeur. You've heard the term, "I could feel the vibes". Well, I really could.

In his acting classes, Clyde often relates moments from our play. He talks of how important it is to listen as an actor. Each night, as he would narrate the story, he found that seeing the photos and video clips, walking through the apartment, and listening to the dramatization from backstage, would move him deeply. By listening to the story being played out, it was only natural for him to walk out on stage and simply tell the truth, as though he were actually me. To portray a part truthfully, an actor must "listen, feel, and react" to everything.

Finally it was opening night that warm day in June 2007 and as I said before it was a huge success. I was called on stage and took that life changing bow I spoke of earlier with the whole cast and we were holding hands joined together in a bond that had taken months to form. I can't describe how great that was. I often tell Clyde, I can't wait to do that again.

Then came good reviews form Martin Brady of the *Nashville Scene* and an article by Fiona Soltes of *The Tennessean* along with an interview by Nick Beres on a local TV show. For me, Peter "Otto" Abeles, thought painful at times, it was one of the biggest thrills of my life. I had bared my soul in public, the good, the bad and the ugly. But I was a better man for it. I found myself profusely thanking everyone involved who had given me this gift, one that truly keeps on giving. In my living room in Bethesda hangs an autographed poster signed by the entire cast and it rekindles the memory every time I walk by it.

In 2008, my friend, Bill Klauber, wrote a column about me in the Pelican Bay Journal. It was a profile piece entitled *Peter Otto Abeles...Reflections from Life under the Nazi Regime*. Bill discussed my book and the play and sponsored me in becoming a member of the Pelican Bay Press Club. His quote reflects how I feel and how each of us should use the talent we have been given. He says: "I had a wonderful and exciting career. When I retired, I pledged to put my time and effort into causes that would benefit others. I believe I have accomplished this and hopefully I'm not through yet." I am so immensely grateful to everyone and so my message to you is simple but profound. Please let people help you. Good people want to help. Don't be afraid to ask. And then be grateful when they do and never forget because remembering is a beautiful thing, a rebirth of sorts. I end with this beautiful sentiment-

We thank You, O God of life and love,
For the resurrecting gift of memory
Which endows your children,
Fashioned in Your image,
With the Godlike sovereign power
To give immortality through love.
Blessed are You, God,
Who enables Your children to remember. –Rabbi Morris Adler

"May your pockets be heavy and your heart be light
May good luck pursue you each morning and night.'

-Universal Irish Toast -

...we all agree sometimes it's better to be lucky than good.

Chapter 28
Catawampus

There are a lot of times when things get a little funny. People express this weirdness in many ways. I am currently a little catawampus myself. You know…slightly askew, a little awry and diagonally opposed to something. Straight lines have rarely been a part of my journey. So I am not uncomfortable in my catawampus. I felt catawampus the first time I saw the Statue of Liberty and suddenly realized I had to learn to speak English.

Tom often speaks in his Southern way of being *kitty corner* yet another way to describe things that are diagonally opposed. In our many variations, we are all in one way or the other a little cater-cornered, kitty-cornered, cata-cornered, and cater-cornered, or cattywampused.

Angularly speaking, we are all quite out of line. Now I say and do and read a multitude of things. Some of it sticks, some of it gets a sigh and a "hmmm", and some of it gets a "no bloody way". Regardless I still read because whether I agree or disagree, it all informs you who I am. I stack my books around me or give them away but words still keep piling up in my journey.

Words are in fact as important as steps. You should have seen me trying to tell someone I needed a restroom my first day of school in Chicago and not speaking the language. It's strange how that event shaped me and how it is etched in my mind.

Each word leads to another and every sentence becomes a paragraph and then a page and there's a book and ultimately my little section ends up in the library of this experience. Curiosity breeds that kind of "snowball" effect as we follow the Universal Syntax. When we actually learn to really communicate then and only then is real peace a possibility.

Like the time I learned a little lesson about bill collection from the business wizard, my former boss, Wayne Huizenga. We were on the road together making calls and he said to me, "I have a bill to collect." I readily agreed. We stopped at a small diner and when we walked in the owner asked, "Are you here again?" Wayne walked over to him and grabbed him "by the balls" and said, "I'm not letting go until you pay me." He paid.

Tom told me a tale once about how silence is sometimes the best way to get a point across. "As a hitchhiking student with a backpack and a trusty thumb, I learned to keep quiet. I endured all kinds of vehicular experiences and always kept my mouth shut because there was an implied option to get out and walk. Later when I had a few nickels to rub together, I had this penchant for finicky vehicles and they tended to break down in remote locations. I still found myself hitching a few rides or after the advent of the cell phone, riding with 'tobacco chewing snuff dippin' tow truck drivers. Again, I kept my mouth shut and the 'any port in a storm' theory prevailed. Chewers allow you to fire up a nice Dominican cigar while you ride. Further episodes included voyages to hospitals like after a misfortune at an intersection in Niles, IL near that little imitation of the tower of Pisa. After being T-boned in an accident, as a passenger in an ambulance, I created great road stories and indulged that kiss Mother Earth feeling of happy to be alive. Yep, I remember the old Plymouth of my youth and how I laid in the rear window sans seatbelt and read my comic books as the old man fired up cigarette after cigarette and sang Hank Williams tunes and listened to my mom nag at him about his driving and I honestly don't think he heard a damn word cause he always smiled like a possum and weaved merrily along doing things his own way. I'm not saying always the right way but always his way."

For all you wannabe writers I present the great Jack Kerouac's "Belief and Technique for Modern Prose'. It is a bit of good advice on waking up the literary genius inside you. It has worked for Tom and me and there is nothing we could add except take the advice of someone who has been on down the road before you. Tell your story. It is in you and waiting to be unveiled just like mine.

1. *Scribbled secret notebooks, and wild typewritten pages, for your own joy*
2. *Submissive to everything, open, listening*
3. *Try never get drunk outside your own house*
4. *Be in love with your life*
5. *Something that you feel will find its own form*
6. *Be crazy dumb saint of the mind*
7. *Blow as deep as you want to blow*
8. *Write what you want bottomless from bottom of the mind*
9. *The unspeakable visions of the individual*
10. *No time for poetry but exactly what is*
11. *Visionary tics shivering in the chest*
12. *In tranced fixation dreaming upon object before you*
13. *Remove literary, grammatical and syntactical inhibition*
14. *Like Proust be an old teahead of time*
15. *Telling the true story of the world in interior monolog*
16. *The jewel center of interest is the eye within the eye*

17. Write in recollection and amazement for yourself

18. Work from pithy middle eye out, swimming in language sea

19. Accept loss forever

20. Believe in the holy contour of life

21. Struggle to sketch the flow that already exists intact in mind

22. Don't think of words when you stop but to see picture better

23. Keep track of every day the date emblazoned in yr morning

24. No fear or shame in the dignity of yr experience, language & knowledge

25. Write for the world to read and see yr exact pictures of it

26. Bookmovie is the movie in words, the visual American form

27. In praise of Character in the Bleak inhuman Loneliness

28. Composing wild, undisciplined, pure, coming in from under, crazier the better

29. You're a Genius all the time

30. Writer-Director of Earthly movies Sponsored & Angeled in Heaven

I truly hope that you always share with others all that you have discovered for as that old Jewish adage states "as you teach you learn" and there's no better way to learn than to teach.

I am continuing to get my education in that old school
of hard knocks every day.
Here I am both a professor and a full time student.
A lifetime of learning is the key to success.

- Otto on turning 80 and adding he has *50 good years
left in him*

Chapter 29
Paine and Endless Pain

My father's friend in Vienna, Eric Kolb, was a man of extraordinary courage. He had *street smarts* before it was called that. It seems he was ordered by the Gestapo to report to their headquarters. He ignored the letter. He told my stunned father that what they would do if he turned himself in was worse than the punishment for ignoring it. He found a way to get out of the country and I think that inspired my father to do the same. Now Tom Paine also had common sense when he wrote *Common Sense* and we think alike in describing the way things are. "The world is my country, all mankind are my brethren, and to do *good* is my religion," Mr. Paine said it and I agree in principle on this practical approach. In 1776, Thomas Paine's pamphlet, *Common Sense* contested the authority of the British government. The plain language that Paine used spoke to the common people of America and was the first work to openly ask for independence.

Now Hickey's mom always told him to use a little common sense. I thought I would try and get a little from Paine. So I decided to have a little conversation in my head and used Paine's words to respond. It is prudent to take some advice from a wise person from the past. That makes a lot of sense to me today.

What say you to people who don't make sense?

To argue with a person who has renounced the use of reason is like administering medicine to the dead.

With you it seems to be best to keep things on an even keel?

A thing moderately good is not so good as it ought to be. Moderation in temper is always a virtue, but moderation in principle is always a vice.

Does modern society get it?

Society is produced by our wants and government by our wickedness.

Explain.

What we obtain too cheap, we esteem too lightly.

So you fight when the cause is right.

When my country, into which I had just set my foot, was set on fire about my ears, it was time to stir. It was time for every man to stir.

As parents, we want to give our children everything they need but despite that we can't live their lives for them, can we?

When we are planning for posterity, we ought to remember that virtue is not hereditary.

In my time, I find very few people who want to set aside time to explore the depths of the human experience and to associate with people of integrity rather than status. One of the things I love about my friends in Florida and my friends in the Washington area is their integrity.

Better fare hard with good men than feast with bad.

The embracing of that which I believe to be Truth is the goal of my life. Why is it so compelling?

Such is the irresistible nature of truth that all it asks, and all it wants, is the liberty of appearing.

Now my mood becomes sullen. Freedom is in short supply worldwide. Slavery is not dead. Not by a long shot, Mr. Paine. *"It has been estimated by World Vision that two million children are enslaved in the global commercial sex trade.* Here's what they write. "Many of these children are either sold into prostitution to pay off family debts or forcibly recruited on the street to work in brothels, where they are required to have sex with as many as 30 men each day. Some prostituted children are just 5 years old. (And this next factoid really pisses me off.)

"United States citizens are among those from several wealthy countries who exploit children trapped in the commercial sex trade and fuel a demand for younger children. Some Americans take advantage of prostituted children while traveling to impoverished countries for business, tourism and other legitimate reasons. Others travel abroad specifically for a "sex tour…Sex tourists travel to countries such as *Cambodia, Thailand, Costa Rica, Mexico and Brazil,* expecting anonymity, low-cost prostitution, easily accessible children and impunity from prosecution. Notably, it is estimated that *one-third of the prostitutes in Cambodia are children."*(Slavery in the 21st Century/ World Vision)

Tom Paine and I have tears rolling down our cheeks. As bad as I suffered, there are children around the world who are suffering far worse and we have supposedly advanced so much. I reached deep to find something that would make sense after 200+ years and then I found it. Those words of Paine's are as profound today as the day they were first spoken.

These are the times that try men's souls.

"Undeniably," I whisper as my blood boils with the same passion now that I am 80 as it did when I was 20 and as it has for freedom fighters in the past like my brother. I was again reminded how Heinz Robert, a new citizen, joined the army of his adopted country and as a part of military intelligence helped capture Axis Sally, the propagandist for the Nazis. He had guts, determination and common sense, a winning combination. If Tom Paine was here right now, he would use his own persuasive words to give us all a pep talk about how we had to be vigilant.

Tyranny, like hell, is not easily conquered.

"C'mon, old friend.
Common Sense is in short supply these days.
There's lots of work to do."

-Otto's reflections on American Patriot Tom Paine

Chapter 30
Unfinished Business

Have you ever felt when you awakened that you had a little unfinished business? Hmmm- Let's see. What do I need to do? Make some fresh coffee. Good for openers. Clip the nose hairs. That's a good idea. Work on that hanging business deal. That's a must do along with establishing mutually beneficial relationships that are only limited by imagination and determination.

Ah, yes, that's it; the plight of humans is to solve all of those little issues that appear on yellow sticky notes and on your smart phone calendar. But as you guess, I can't leave it hanging like that for there is that looming philosophical life question that needs to be answered. I wasn't about to let something as complicated as life be that easy. In your heart, you know it's not. There's an urge kind of like that unfinished business feeling that keeps you on your toes.

Well now Tom speaks often of the rather obscure Arnold Geulincx who did have such an urge and his question was a piece of unfinished business that to him was left in an obscure and unsatisfactory state by none other than Descartes of Cogito ergo sum fame:

I think therefore I am.

Whereas Descartes made the union of soul and body rather a violent marriage, Geulincx practically called the union a miracle. Sometimes you can over-think and worry and the results are the same and usually things work out and you can't quite explain it but you just pick up the pieces and move on. As the old Jewish proverb declares, "Just as the world cannot exist without livelihoods, so it cannot exist without miracles and wonders." That certainly works for me and hopefully for you.

Back to Arnold, in the late 1600's, Geulincx used the pseudonym Philaretus just like I am Otto and Tom is Hickey and Rodney is Clyde. Anyhow I like that Greek sounding alias and I like this philosopher and logician a lot. Geulincx wrote all his works in Latin, and died before his principal books could be published.

He summarized his philosophy as "Ita est, ergo ita sit", ("it exists, therefore it is so,").

And he believed in a "pre-established harmony" which may have led to Leibniz' philosophy of optimism and the notion of this world as the "best of all possible worlds." You must remember that you have to play the hand you're dealt.

Tom says that Geulincx didn't go that far but instead explained the relationship between mind and body by the analogy of two clocks like the ones in my office that I look at every day to make sure I get where I need to be. You do not ever want to miss something important like a *Tee Time*. When you get to be 80, you love your memory but you can't quite trust it to get you where you need to be.

The internal clocks of your life are synchronized by God at each instant and there is a harmony between them. We often have discussions about how things need to be in "sync" and actually they will set themselves right despite our best efforts to screw them up. I take care of myself and seek to ensure that my body and my mind are together. Having a good spouse and an extended family and good friends are necessary to achieve that end.

Geulincx was important as the precursor of Spinoza and others from the big theoretical perspective but most of us are hitting the bricks every day and aren't thinking about little known philosophers from the past. Nevertheless as Tom asserts the thing that is more important is that Geulincx chose to be a little obscure, a little different, and be himself.

Perhaps as Tom suggests when we are not awake in our own life experience, the miracles are missed because we, ourselves, are missing from them in our busy lives.

Maybe that's the real unfinished business and that is something to think about. Whether learning something to strengthen my mind or pumping iron to build up my body, no pain equals no gain. I still work out because I know there's always something to gain.

"The Iron never lies to you. You can walk outside and listen to all kinds of talk...
The Iron will always kick you the real deal.
The Iron is the great reference point, the all-knowing perspective giver...
Friends may come and go. But two hundred pounds is always two hundred pounds." -Henry Rollins

Chapter 31
Short Films and Long Lives

When I put on a fresh shirt or I jump into bed between recently changed sheets, I am revived and in the immortal words of Don Quixote: "Todo saldra en al colada." All will come out in the washing.

It is true. Clean things evoke good thoughts and feelings and remind us that most of what life throws at us can be washed away in the cleansing waters of forgiveness.

My mother and I had a challenging relationship and there were episodes that I told about in my first book and in the rest of my story that I revealed in the plays we produced. The most important is the fact that I was able to forgive her even after she had passed away.

That itself was a cleansing and cathartic experience that helped me to learn to love her in ways that I could never have done until I experienced that forgiveness. Remember, there is always more that you can do. It is never too late.

Taking a complex story and making it into a "short" film for the Sundance Film Festival was a challenge but a group of us did it in less than a week. The challenge to make that short film happen was another example of how people working together can do something special.

Another week later, our short film, *Otto's Toy* arrived in L.A. safe and sound ready to view. It was done. We didn't win but it was an opportunity to take the story to another level and infuse some fresh ideas. Remember that all of your ideas don't turn out like you expect them to but that is not an excuse to stop trying.

Ralph Waldo Emerson said, "Finish each day and be done with it. You have done what you could. Some blunders and absurdities no doubt crept in; forget them as soon as you can. Tomorrow is a new day; begin it well and serenely and with too high a spirit to be encumbered with your old nonsense."

A lot of what we humans think and do is nonsense. We need to know it when it happens and not let our spirits be held back by our ego selves. But above all forgive others and then yourself and as soon as possible forget about what doesn't make us stronger and better. I still view that film and it reminds me that Tom and I sponsored a student film festival for two years where we encouraged young people to take their ideas and express them on film. We were blown away by the response and the quality of the films that were submitted to our little festival.

Tom often speaks of his paperback hero, an old beach bum and philosopher character, Travis McGee who spent his money as he made it taking his retirement as he would say "in small chunks" as he went along.

If you are waiting for one big grand finale when you make up for not doing it along the way, you may be surprised to find that things can change quickly and in ways you couldn't have dreamed. People die every day and trust me they weren't intending to; so remember your own vacation land in your dreams and visit there as often as you can.

I also concur with and love an old African tradition that states if you think or dream something then it probably has happened or will happen somewhere, sometime. That works for me because we would be sorely disappointed if all of those wonderful dreams we've had went to waste.

Don't wait for your fate. Create it.

After Otto and I saw Woody Allen's beautiful film *Midnight in Paris*; we became inspired by the spirit of the creative forces that converged in the 1920's in Paris not very far from where young Otto lived in Vienna. The words of Gertrude Stein inspire us on our quest
"If you knew it all it would not be creation but dictation."
I say to all of you build your own device.
— Hickey

Chapter 32
In the Spotlight

Over the years, we have had the opportunity to be on radio and television shows and featured in many newspapers and magazines. I have spoken to women's groups and at arts festivals like the one in Charlotte, NC in 2002. In 2003, I appeared at the Naples Rotary Club and received an American flag that had flown over the White House. I was honored beyond belief. Taking every opportunity to grab the spotlight is imperative in your marketing approach but more importantly it is about making as many people aware of your goal as humanly possible through as many means as you can.

I know that big things come a little bit each day for a reason for to have it instantly or without work would be overwhelming and would not afford me the time to really appreciate its magnitude.

As Jung would say, "Even a happy life cannot be without a measure of darkness, and the word happy would lose its meaning if it were not balanced by sadness. It is far better to take things as they come along with patience and equanimity." That is a good fit and then when they throw the spotlight on you there is a realization that it took a lot of little moments and a lot of good people to get you there on center stage.

My friend, Mort Stein, asked Tom and me to come to Akron, Ohio and appear on his television show Civic Forum of the Air on Time Warner Cable in the fall of 2001, a volatile time in our country's history. I met Mort the year before through a golf buddy of mine. We met and "clicked" and I knew immediately that we would be friends. That led to his kind invitation to appear on his show after I shared my story and told him about the book. Jumping on a plane to make an event is a small price to pay for the chance to spread the word about your projects. You have to keep your efforts and your website fresh. There are lots of things to capture people's attention and you must be special in some way and you must never allow yourself to grow stale.

Anyway as we filmed that first interview in the *Heartland*, I noticed the burly cameraman in a white torn t shirt. As I was telling the story of how my mother tried to get us to commit suicide because of the stress created by the Nazis, he began to cry and I began to cry myself and Tom touched my hand to console me.

As we finished the interview and later viewed it, it became clear to us that the story was both compelling and timely given the current state of affairs.

Six years later in 2007, we returned and gave a second interview in the form of a round table discussion prior to the opening of the stage production and discussed our short film submittal to Sundance Film Festival.

Mort has turned out to be another one of those good friends who helps us at every turn and makes living in this world a pleasure.

It was John Muir who said sadly that *most people are on the world, not in it – having no conscious sympathy or relationship to anything about them – undiffused, separate, and rigidly alone like marbles of polished stone, touching but separate?* I have learned that I am a man not a stone. That's a good thing.

God and all my friends remind me of that daily. Tom feels the same way and told me it came through in a special manner when he was performing in *Fiddler on the Roof* years ago and sang of gazing at the sunset and sunrise in new and different ways.

I am learning to properly gaze. As Mort would say, "Make life a bowl of cherries. Just don't swallow the pits."

"Raising awareness is the first step. Wearing a tux to your opening night comes later."

p.s. Clyde even has a special baseball hat he wears with his tux and Hickey won't even wear socks with his Gucci loafers so I say screw the fashion police when <u>your</u> time comes.

Chapter 33
Old Dreams in a New City

As you get older, you have a tendency to editorialize. I sat down and banged out this story for a local paper after a request for an editorial. As I was reflecting on my new home and came to appreciate that home was anywhere I was and anyplace where I carried the true reserves of my life; that treasure trove within me of a little bit of this and a little bit of that.

As a young boy, my family occupied the third floor of an apartment building on Heiligenstadterstrasse in picturesque Vienna, Austria. In those days in the late 1930's, I spent a great deal of time looking out any available window...wishing, dreaming, reflecting or just observing life.

Things haven't changed much in that regard and fortunately for me, thanks to my father's ingenuity, my family and I were able to escape the Holocaust and start a new life in America. It wasn't long until I learned to speak English and not long after I did when I heard of this beautiful tropical paradise in my new land, called Florida. From my cramped Chicago apartment on snowy nights, I looked out another window and dreamed again of such a wonderful warm place.

Now sixty-nine years later, after a flourishing business career, co-authoring a successful book and co-producing a captivating play about my life with dreams of a future movie, I find myself sitting in my study in beautiful Naples Florida. As I look out the airy window at the Gulf, the beach and the grand skyline, I realize how lucky my family and I are to be able to spend almost six months every year here. I am convinced Naples is one of the most stunning and peaceful spots in the world. I feel I am not being trite when I say I was destined to be here. The word, Naples is derived from the Greek expression that means new city. For me, it was a new city for a new phase of my life. But there can be trouble in paradise.

I chuckle out loud as I think about the gyrations I have to go through to get my wife, Bonnie, to agree on a departure date from our Bethesda, Maryland home as winter approaches. With five grown children and eleven grandchildren, between us, it is always somebody's birthday or anniversary plus Thanksgiving and the December holidays thrown into the mix. I have discovered that she has a lot of plans to implement and she is "always" right.

But like any good businessman, I learn from my past blunders and every year I start the negotiation a little earlier. I can be very shrewd. For instance, being Jewish our life is primarily controlled by guilt. So there is a lot of give and take. The kids and grandchildren "give" the guilt and I "take" a trip southward pointing out that seniors are much healthier out of the cold weather, shivering as I make my case. Finally a date is chosen, the boxes are packed, the car is shipped and we arrive blissfully in Naples. Then it takes us about one day to fall in love again with the beach, the Phil and all the great restaurants. My wife remembers all of her favorite shopping haunts and the retail sector of the community gets an immediate boost as the economy improves.

And then my wife says to me, "Honey, why didn't we come sooner?"

I reply to her that she makes a very good point. After all, she's "always" right.

That article really summed it up for me and the many comments I received were all so positive. I have to admit, I liked it myself. You know, "I've got it good", as they say and even when I didn't have it so "good" I acted as if I did. I suggest you do the same. In other words, fake it 'til you make it. You just never know. And, besides, it feels so good.

"A positive attitude is like a signpost pointing home."

-Otto's quip after leaving Los Angeles and heading back to Chicago

Chapter 34
You can always go back...
Just don't stay there

When my wife Bonnie and I planned our trip to Eastern Europe I had no idea what range of emotions this journey would produce for me and how that would help me produce something positive and productive.

It started out with a feeling of horror. In a surreal few days, there we were in Warsaw visiting the Jewish Ghetto Memorial and my mind's eye produced a vision of the 400,000 people, including 1000 children who were slaughtered there. Then we found ourselves at Auschwitz and the infamous concentration camp followed by the museum. It was a tough decision to visit this site, however family and friends convinced me that it was necessary. Sometimes the only way to find complete healing is to face the pain.

As we toured the site I was like in a trance, I would hear sounds like people screaming, shots being fired, guards yelling, children running and death around me. Though my experience was nothing like this, I returned to the terror I felt as a child in Vienna.

Then I went from terror to awe for as the trip continued we visited many beautiful and historic sites in Poland. We traveled through the scenic Tatra Mountains, located in both Slovakia and Poland en route to Hungary and Austria. I wondered if my father's Tatra automobile was named after those mountains.

As we neared Austria and Vienna my thoughts were on our planned visit to the old neighborhood in Vienna and the apartment we had left to escape from the Holocaust. I was sure that I would recognize the area and the building. I was both scared and excited and even contemplated not going at all. I recalled a piece of advice someone once gave. "You can never go back."

Finally the day arrived. It was September 6, 2008. My wife Bonnie and I, with our four friends, got directions and boarded the street car. We were on our way and the memory floodgate opened. I remembered once again how my father devised a plan to get us out of the country, how we sadly had to leave my beloved Grandmother behind, and how we managed to get on the last boat to leave Holland. All real, yet it was all so dreamlike.

As we were discussing our plans a young lady whom I will always remember as our Guardian Angel apparently overheard our conversation and asked if she could help. Her name was Agnes Eigner. She was a law student who had nearly completed her studies.

We answered *yes*, emphatically, and I gave her the address. She looked at it and said "oh my you've just passed your stop, you must get off now."

We got off at the next stop and started walking back toward our address. We were quite a group. The closer we got, the stranger I felt. It all began to look familiar and all at once I yelled, "There it is, my building."

I realized it looked exactly as I had described it to the playwright of our play "Otto". We started ringing door bells and finally someone let us in. We knocked on the door of my early home and explained our mission to the elderly lady who answered the door. At first she was hesitant but when she finally understood, she let us in. Now here I was, 69 years later, in the home of my youth.

After taking several pictures, I asked if I could stand in front of "my window" and look out. Memories totally overwhelmed me as I peered out that window. I looked across the street and all at once I had a vision of what I saw as a young child looking out the window in March 1938. The majority of the people had Nazi flags hanging out their windows and I could see the faces of the people as they listened to a loudspeaker telling them that Hitler had taken over Austria. I stood there as long as I dared, realizing that another chapter in my life was closing while one was yet to be read.

We may choose to be the birthplace of our endless wishes as they present themselves to us. Or better yet we may learn what it means to let the part of the past die that needs to be given a real birth into a new and better life. I seek that higher dimension of existence and suggest you do the same.

Don't expect to ever do anything right the first time. To make a mistake is not wrong but to not take the time to improve or correct it makes no sense. The fact that my neighbors in Vienna let me down reinforced the fact that I should be a good neighbor.

After going through the experience of revisiting my childhood home I came to fully understand how my father at first refused to leave until he realized he had to leave. Sometimes we don't understand what motivates other people. In fact, we many times misunderstand them and often judge them prematurely.

Always be tolerant of other people's needs and dreams and always try to support their plans as much as your own. I have learned that sometimes we all need a partner.

I live wherever I am. My address is inside me.

-Otto upon returning to his boyhood home in Vienna
"Heiligenstädter Strasse"

"One day, in retrospect, the years of struggle will strike you as the most beautiful."
— Sigmund Freud
A former resident of Vienna who grew up in the Jewish neighborhood of Leopoldstadt near my grandmother's home

Chapter 35
A Reality of Beauty

While watching Tom twirling the stalk of celery in his Bloody Mary on a road trip, I thought of Ontology, of objects and their relationship. The unraveling of the theory gives us information for providing distinction for types of objects, such as concrete and abstract or existent and non-existent, real and ideal, independent and dependent and their ties.

Now it can be simple or it can be complicated but you have to always be looking for the connection between things. I learned at a very early age that the tie between gravity and me is that if I don't watch my step, I would fall down and skin my knee. And if I made my mother Karla angry, she would have my father punish me and this was often very hurtful. I have always preached to my children and grandchildren that every decision they make has a definite consequence whether they accept it or not.

Some philosophers, such as Plato and his heady bunch, generally thought that all nouns refer to entities. Other thinkers surmised that some nouns do not name entities but provide a kind of shorthand way of referring to a collection of either objects or the events surrounding them. I could never separate the people from the events in my early years. I am getting better at that as the years go on. But it's hard to do.

Tom is an old Parrothead and listens to the song *Defying Gravity* by Jimmy Buffett a lot and loves to take me to Margaritaville in Nashville. I wish I could defy gravity sometimes but alas I am a law abiding chap, even if it's Newton's Law.

When you head out on a new adventure, it is certainly helpful to know where the heck you are going or at least with the help of your Atlas or compass or GPS, the general direction in which you are moving, but don't forget: the only thing that is real about your trip is the step that you are taking at this exact second. That's all there ever really is. Getting beyond that is sometimes getting ahead of your own self which sets you back. As Clyde would say backward is forward in reverse.

Tom and I have tried some business ventures that were absolute failures. I have often heard the phrase "That's just not fair". Fairness in "flawed me" is an ideal and I fall short on implementation of it personally as I do in many things as a human.

I probably would not have wished for some of the things that have happened to me and neither would you. Justice is indeed one of those mysteries that you might be unable to explain at the moment. In the world we live in thoughts in the end can't be kept secret and what I think I am is who I am and the unfolding circumstances of my life can change a lot of things but I am what I think I am and I shall not leave my self-image up to anyone else. My father thought the Nazis would not bother him if he minded his own business and he learned the hard way that they had another agenda altogether.

That is why we should honor the "composer, sculptor, painter, poet, prophet, and sage" who gives us a vision of what this world should really be like. Their ideas of beauty become the reality of beauty for us. We can do the same for others by how we live our lives. Gravity might cause me to fall but there are other forces that help me get up again and right now I am able to stand if I choose.

I hope that my examples have demonstrated that I volunteered to sacrifice and pursue my worthy goals. To an outsider it may look like good fortune comes easy but it is the realization of our lifelong dreams that entered us first in thought and then in deeds and required a sacrifice of the most valuable resource we have and that is our limited amount of time on earth.

PROSIT! To A Full Glass of New Goals!

-Otto on deciding to write his second book

Chapter 36
Write a few notes

John Locke's blank slate, the *tabula rasa*, is that consciousness slate on which the self begins to be written and is not unlike another blank slate, the old chalkboard in my grade school classroom, where I continued my quest to find out if I had it in me to learn the English language. I did. No one can tell the difference now. In fact, it's my German that is suspect.

There was a time when a person was judged on their handwriting. I have tried to make sure my writing skills were acceptable. In the old days, it could get me a slap across the face from my mother. There is a certain beauty in writing in longhand after stroking the keyboard of a desktop all week. With ordinary, cursive handwriting the best speed of writing is about 35 words per minute compared to typing which according to some experts are about 50 words per minute. But here again it is not about mere speed, but more the individual beauty and uniqueness of handwriting.

In the play, *Bad Seed*, 10 year old Rhoda Penmark was so distraught about losing the penmanship award to Claude Daigle she took it upon herself to take it from him, before killing him. I don't take my penmanship that seriously.

When I came to America I took reading, writing, and arithmetic seriously. I knew I had to learn to survive. One of my early teachers in Chicago told the class one day that all of her ancestors came over on the Mayflower and looked toward me for a response. I was hurt but I answered her which took all of the courage I could muster and I answered truthfully in my broken English. I said that was very good. But my family had to take a mental competency test to enter. I was proud of myself.

When I got home I told Heinz Robert the story and as usual he was encouraging and said I did the right thing by honestly answering her and not getting angry. We did our own special handshake and just touching my brother made things better.

After thousands of years it is still about human touch. Researchers in Utah found that a warm touch — the non-sexual supportive kind which may surprise screenwriters and novelists — tempers stress and blood pressure, adding to a growing body of research on how emotions affect health. The study found that supportive and caring touch lowers stress hormones and blood pressure. Can a piece of molded plastic wrapped around a computer chip do that for you?

So on your blank slate; write a note to yourself to write a note to someone else. It's a great idea to keep track of important things you learn as you go. Lloyd, who is now president of Flom Corporation, started out learning this business from the ground up. After working at a waste paper sorting plant in Alexandria, Virginia, he then went to White Pigeon Paper Company, a paper mill that utilizes waste paper instead of pulp to make their product. Lloyd learned what happens if contaminated paper is not sorted properly. At the end of this learning period he told me he was sure glad he went to college as he looked at the cuts on his hands. I am glad I met him and even happier that he became my son in law as he has been the driving force of Flom's growth and success.

Our lives are a tablet on which we write our story. We are not born a winner or a loser. We are born a chooser. My prayer for you the reader is that you choose wisely. I haven't always chosen wisely and discovered there is a price to pay for your mistakes but a small price compared to the joy of your successes!

Take notes about your own life and
Then post those on the big board called …My Legacy

"That reminds me," Clyde said, "I used to use post-it
notes as reminders …but could never remember where
I posted them."

Chapter 37
Try on a few hats for size

I am a negotiator and as I alluded to earlier I learned a lot of those skills from Ed Law, my business partner of many years. I like to be more than talk for there is that time lag between what you are and what you profess to be. If you *talk the talk you better walk the walk*. Remember my earlier lesson about connectivity of the real and the ideal.

Now talk is, in fact cheap, but truth is in fact rare and valuable. Flex your muscle with concise and clear comments. Be passionate but name calling and raw untamed emotion looks and often is distracting and counter-productive.

It is rumored that on a $50 bet that a book couldn't be written with 50 words and as a result "Green Eggs and Ham" was born. Who knows about the truth of this report but regardless the use of a few "selective" rhyming words to make profound statements about the pressing political and social issues that face us is the stuff I choose to call pure genius.

Is it important what or who things are called? For the good doctor has reportedly said "Seuss rhymes with voice". All of us generally pronounced it in English with an initial s sound and rhyming with "juice". The "Dr." in his pen name is an acknowledgment of his father's unfulfilled hopes that Seuss would earn a doctorate at Oxford. I am glad he stuck to making words a way to heal all of our spirits. Tom has appeared as Yertle the Turtle on stage and a huge fan of Dr. Seuss. He thinks there is a lot of good sound business advice in those "children's" books. I love them, too. I read the stories to my grandchildren.

Now Tom has a few thoughts on this subject on the use of words and images that he wrote about in his book, The Philosophy of Tommy Typical. In this case, it happens to be the proverbial hat:

To lie is akin to talking through your hat. If you agree in advance to eat your hat, you're probably betting on a sure thing. If it's old hat, it's out of style. If you're mad as a hatter, you're suffering from a brain disorder because hat makers worked with dangerous fumes and were often thought to be drunk. If you arrive with your hat in hand, you're being contrite and humble. Passing the hat means you're looking for a hand-out or contribution.

If something is as tight as Dick's hat band, it's just, well, too tight, like the original Dick, aka Richard Cromwell, who's hat was the crown of England, one he didn't get to wear. If you get three goals in a game, you get a hat trick. If you want to run for office, you throw your hat in the ring. Hat's off for kudos. A feather in your cap is an achievement and the list goes on and on proving that we can wear many hats real and figuratively and you can hang your hat on that.

Yes, indeed, we all wear many hats and we all say many things trying to get our point across and come out on top as we negotiate our way through life with a smile on our faces because nobody likes an old grouch and a whiner and that is why I make every effort to abide by the old Jewish proverb "Never trust the man who tells you all his troubles but keeps from you all his joys."

I began wearing hats after going to my first baseball game in 1940. You may remember that I had to wear bobby pins in my hair when I first came to America to keep the hair out of my eyes. It wasn't easy being a kid in Chicago and wearing those bobby pins along with my strange European clothing. My first hat was blue with a red "C" and it was a symbol of the boy I had become and the man I would one day be. Whatever hat you wear, wear it with pride!

"There's no end to the number of hats you can wear in your life or the number of occasions when you can muster an award winning smile."

Clyde alleges, "I'll wear any hat as long as it's a Cardinal hat."

Chapter 38
Things of Great Import

It's not all about me by any stretch of the imagination. Because behind every "man at the wheel" there is the "boy at the pump" filling up for the long ride. For me, that has been my son-in-law Lloyd whom I mentioned earlier. For the last 20 years, he has taken our company and through his own time and investment has made it stronger and better than I could have ever dreamed.

We have weathered several economic downturns and we continue to find ways to reinvent ourselves through creative financing and marketing. And we are all about face to face meetings and honoring our contracts through "thick and thin." Always evaluate your business in the light of the long term.

We attach ourselves to growing companies and become a part of their growth and when we use the term partner in our customer references we mean it. I truly believe that is one of the big reasons we continue to be successful.

We have taken many companies from thinking of their waste as a disposable item to a consistent revenue stream that is a "green" pay-off in terms of recycling. All the while they improve the cleanliness and the efficiency of their operations. It is hard to express how gratifying that truly is.

And nothing means more to me than when Lloyd and Tom come to me for advice. I love the times when things that I have learned throughout the years are useful to these guys. Sometimes Clyde will call me in the evening to ask my advice and to talk baseball. It chokes me up when he tells me how much respect he has for me. Little does he know how much respect I have for him.

All these guys teach me something new every day as well. Just the other day, I was reading a note from Tom that he posted to *Peterman's Eye*, advertised as a community of curious travelers. (We both wear our Picasso shirts from J Peterman)-

Boredom is a little pathetic and quite egotistical. Planned Laziness on the other hand is a true art form practiced in places like hammocks or on beach towels where carnal and spiritual pleasures are derived from cheating the system of mindless activity and seeking the transcendence of doing nothing with great intent.

At such times, one blows on a daffodil, sucks the juice out of a honeysuckle, cloud watches, chews and pops bubble gum, hums to the tune of old rockabilly classics and forgives oneself of this and that thought or activity - things of great import.

There's a rather famous saying that has often been attributed to John Lennon and Laurence J. Peter, and because of a mistake, even Bertrand Russell. Actually the earliest known user of the phrase was novelist Marthe Troly-Curtin and it goes something like this. "Time you enjoy wasting is not wasted time."

Now I never really thought of laziness as a positive trait but Tom has taught me that even something with negative connotations can be turned into something constructive.

Every project requires tools, a big measuring stick, and
a six pack of inspiration

Chapter 39
That's the way the ball bounces

During one of our fundraisers to make a documentary, we were just getting started and our friend, Liliana asked us to go see Joseph Newgarden, a distinguished gentleman who came to see our play. He was an amazing man and gave us one of our first donations.

Joe Newgarden is the President, Owner and Founder of Newgy Industries, Inc. and inventor of the Robo-Pong. Joe is a lifelong table tennis enthusiast and was inducted into the Table Tennis Hall of Fame in 2007 for his commitment and generosity to the sport. Mr. Newgarden started working on the table tennis robot as a hobby in 1972. Three years later his hobby became a business. The table tennis robot took 16 years of research and development before its first commercial release in 1988. Robo-Pong® debuted to rave reviews from the table tennis community. It is a pattern that has continued with each new generation of Robo-Pong table tennis robots.

It takes one to know one, we always say and Tom and I were impressed by his entrepreneurial spirit and his desire to help us got the ball rolling. Leave it to Liliana Kohann to know a man such as this for she came to America from Poland and saw nothing but opportunity. She is willing and able to try anything and has one of the most talented families I've ever met.

Talent may be in the DNA but raw talent alone is not enough to get things done.

Tom says that all the boys in his group carried their ball glove on the handlebars of their bike and kept their Zebco rod and reel in a place where they could snatch it without anyone noticing and they all carried their marbles in a bag in their pocket next to their Barlow knife so they could find a good place to draw a circle and play a game. The prized cat's eye was like Indiana Jones exotic prized jewel. The chalk was absconded from the school tray at the bottom of the Chalkboard next to the erasers after you de-hexed it because the teacher may have used it for those long "long division" problems that started at the top and went all the way to the bottom of the board and therefore cursed it. Playing marbles like most things took skill and talent but also took a little luck.

He goes on to say as a kid, your stuff defined you as you defined it. There is a fine line between matter and thought. We are taught quantum physics without ever entering a classroom. We should try to teach children that being alert to your senses and observing and connecting is a big part of education. There's nothing wrong with looks and talent but it's what's inside that counts.

Once I worked for a Commodities Trader in Chicago on LaSalle Street. I pulled the ticker tape that came through the wall and we tried to keep up with the price changes. When the market became volatile, the tape moved so fast that we couldn't keep up with it. We just put a waste basket beneath it and let the basket fill up. When we would see a symbol that we knew would spike the interest of one of the traders we liked, we would snatch it and run to tell him because it could mean a cash reward. Sometimes our tips would be worth more than the job we were paid to do and that business skills were important but being shrewd was equally if not more fruitful.

Later I worked at the Merchandise Mart at a hosiery company and I worked in the packing room. I didn't much like it except there was a shortage of nylons at the time and one of the fringe benefits was two pairs of nylons twice a week to take home. This greatly enhanced my love life. Sometimes talent is good but sometimes you just stumble onto a good thing. When the universe offers you a gift, take it. As the old Jewish saying goes, when someone gives you something, take it and when someone takes something, scream. I don't like to scream!

Serve it up and when your opponent makes a bad shot, take him out.
You can kiss and make up later.

Clyde says, "A good competitor makes his own breaks."

Hickey says, "Clyde makes his own breaks all right. Lunch breaks."

Chapter 40
King me

In the movie, *Bucket List*, Academy Award winning actors Morgan Freeman and Jack Nicholson play two characters that set out on a road trip with a wish list of things to do before they leave this planet. They go skydiving together, climb the Pyramids, drive a Shelby Mustang, fly over the North Pole, eat dinner at Chevre d'Or in France, visit and praise the beauty and history of Taj Mahal, India, ride motorcycles on the Great Wall of China, and attend a lion safari in Africa. They confide in each other all things personal concerning faith, beliefs, and even regrets. In the end, they discover what's really important.

Clyde reminded us as he always does of a country song by Tim McGraw, son of pitching great, Tug McGraw. It's about a man who seeks adventure and discovers that you should live as if time is your most valuable commodity. It is.

So, live each day as though it were your last. I like being the man at the wheel but if you must know, it still gets scary sometimes. The older you get, the more you worry about falling or worse. You are proud of all you've done but also sad for what you might not get to do. So you cram in as much as you can.

Be ready for criticism no matter what you do but if you can't take a little of that crap, then you don't have much backbone anyway.

The best way to care is to not give a damn. I'm not speaking about people but about the everyday trivial things that can drag you down as you go driving along.

And sometimes you find a wide open spot and you don't see anyone else around and you mash that accelerator and let it roll.

We all like to be cautious but there are times when you haul ass. That's why I bought a Corvette. It is fast and it is ostentatious and it says "Look at me! I not only get there, I get there in style."

Look, if you are not your greatest admirer then tell me who that might be. When I stood at that window in Vienna looking at marching Nazis and when I rode on that train through Holland, believe me I was scared. But I also discovered something deep inside of me and that was the confidence I would get through all of this. I became my own hero at eight and remain so at eighty.

Tom is always touting Maslow. He often quotes him to me and Maslow is famous for his *hierarchy of needs.* The bottom line is once you feed and clothe yourself, then it's high time to shoot for the moon. If you fall short, you're still among the stars.

One of Tom's favorite *Maslowisms* is:

"One's only rival is one's own potentialities. One's only failure is failing to live up to one's own possibilities. In this sense, every man can be a king, and must therefore be treated like a king."

In his movie *History of the World, Part 1* the inimitable Mel Brooks said, "It's good to be king". I say he is right. Like in the game of checkers when you finally reach that goal of the last row, you say "King Me", let it be said, Otto likes to dine with other self-appointed Kings and Queens. Care to join me?

You are King of your own kingdom.
Treat yourself like royalty.

Last Call

Well, there you have it 40 short chapters written about a man of few words with many dreams. For you, the reader, we present our 40 lessons which contain an exponential number of hidden blessings. For as I stated with each trial and challenge there are blessings attached. There is growth involved. There is ancient and enduring knowledge to guide you. I am "the man at the wheel" an emigrant in a garbage truck built by this great country's manufacturers and inventors and continually fueled by other workers' liberality who have said to me overtly and indirectly "just keep rolling, Otto until you pass that finish line with a wad of cash in your hand and a grin on your face." Thanks to Tom and Clyde who stuck out their thumbs and shared part of the ride with me and helped me tell this story. In the end, they will jump off and hop behind their own wheels just like you will and then we will roar down the road together to that future that we have collectively dreamed up and knew one day would come to be. We will all meet up at Otto's Place and share a few cold ones and some stories about life and love and kicking some ass and getting our ass kicked a few times. Yes, that little boy "Otto at the window" now has a hero to watch and it is him all grown up as "Otto, The Man at the Wheel." He's not perfect but he's all I got. Remember you are all you got. Love yourself and you will find it's the first step in truly loving others.

Shalom,

Peter "Otto" Abeles   Tom Hicks   Rodney Pickel

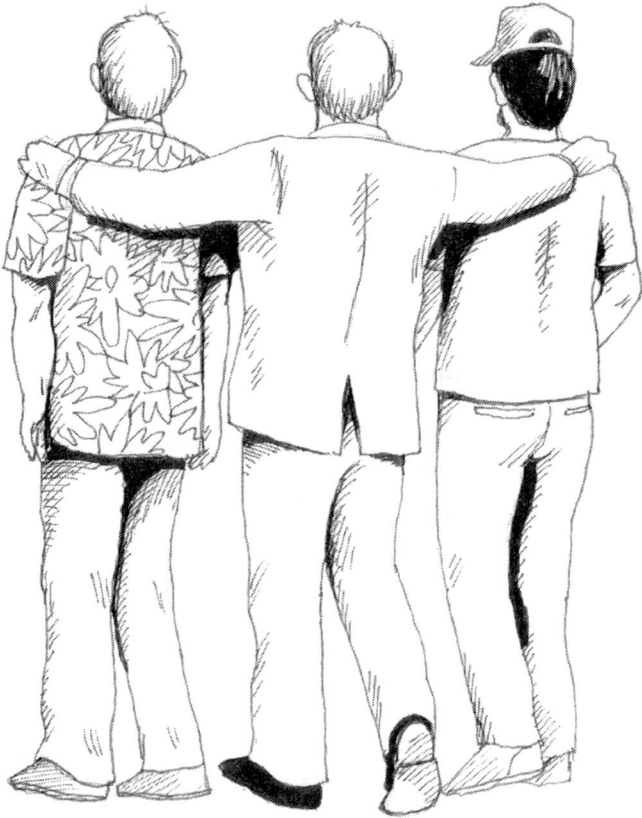

Remember boys, if you can grow up to be your own
hero,

You have achieved the American Dream, too.

CPSIA information can be obtained at www.ICGtesting.com
Printed in the USA
LVOW121338050212

267148LV00001B/2/P